ANOTHER
CHANCE
FOR
LOVE

ANOTHER CHANCE FOR LOVE

Finding a Partner Later in Life

By Sol Gordon, Ph.D.,
and Elaine Fantle Shimberg

Adams Media
Avon, Massachusetts

Published by
Adams Media, an F+W Publications Company
57 Littlefield Street, Avon, MA 02322. U.S.A.
www.adamsmedia.com

ISBN: 1-59337-006-7

Printed in the United States of America.

J   I   H   G   F   E   D   C   B   A

Library of Congress Cataloging-in-Publication Data
Gordon, Sol
Another chance for love / Sol Gordon and Elaine Fantle Shimberg.
p.   cm.
Includes index.
ISBN 1-59337-006-7
1. Dating (Social customs) 2. Love. 3. Intimacy (Psychology)
4. Middle aged persons—Psychology. I. Shimberg, Elaine Fantle II. Title.
HQ801.G5943 2004
646.7'7—dc22
2003022595

This publication is designed to provide accurate and authoritative information with regard to
the subject matter covered. It is sold with the understanding that the publisher is not engaged
in rendering legal, accounting, or other professional advice. If legal advice or other expert
assistance is required, the services of a competent professional person should be sought.
—From a *Declaration of Principles* jointly adopted by a Committee of the American Bar
Association and a Committee of Publishers and Associations

Many of the designations used by manufacturers and sellers to distinguish their
products are claimed as trademarks. Where those designations appear in this book and
Adams Media was aware of a trademark claim, the designations have been printed in
initial capital letters.

"Late Love" by Judith Viorst. From *Suddenly Sixty and Other Shocks of Later Life*.
Published by Simon & Schuster. Copyright ©2000 by Judith Viorst. Reprinted by permission of Lescher & Lescher, Ltd. All rights reserved.

"Dr. Fun's Mass Media Love Quiz" on page 72 is from *Sex, Love, and Romance in the Mass
Media: Analysis and Criticism of Unrealistic Portrayals and Their Influence* by Dr. Mary
Lou Galician, and is used with permission.

Cover illustration ©Thinkstock/Superstock.

*This book is available at quantity discounts for bulk purchases.
For information, call 1-800-872-5627.*

Late Love
By Judith Viorst

He dies.
She dies.
And after great loneliness
Those who are left behind
Find each other,
Or redefine each other
From neighbor or old friends
To companion,
Intimate.
And, most amazingly,
Lover . . .

Dedication

My voice in this book is dedicated to the blessed memory of my wife and best friend, Judith, who died of cancer on November 12, 1991.

It is also dedicated to my very dear friend and current partner, Marlene Appley, and to my dearest sister, Ethel Schnipper, who I love and admire for her loyalty, dedication to family, and her resilience.

Sol Gordon

I dedicate this work to Faith (Remember the bat!).

Elaine Fantle Shimberg

Contents

Acknowledgments

We are especially grateful to the many men and women who shared their experiences on taking another chance for love and of their same-gender and other-gender friendships. Out of respect for their privacy, we have, by their request, used only their initials or a fictitious first name. But the anecdotes attributed to them are their actual comments. We feel their input should add a great deal of encouragement to others who walk the same scary and sometimes lonely path until taking a chance on love.

Thanks also to Veronica Tillis, who helped proofread our initial manuscript. Any typos still there are ours alone.

We also are grateful to a lovely, bright, and clever woman and friend, Judith Viorst. And, of course, we sincerely appreciate the efforts of our agent, Faith Hamlin, and our editor, Danielle Chiotti, and thank them for their friendship, their interest in our work, and timely suggestions.

Introduction

"However rare true love may be,
it is still less so than genuine friendship."

—Duc François de La Rochefoucauld (1613–1680),
French author and moralist

SO, YOU'RE SINGLE . . . AGAIN. Or perhaps you've always been and would like to find a companion, though not necessarily in marriage. Then this book is for you. So jump in—the water's fine.

You may feel nervous about "going through all that dating stuff again." You may figure you're too old. Well, we have news for you. It ain't over yet! And you're hardly alone. There are some 35 million singles age forty plus in America who are seeking a new and happy life, almost all of whom have experienced disappointing or disastrous experiences of failed marriages, love affairs, and romances. *Another Chance for Love* tells why the key is *not* focusing on falling in love again.

Take Your Time

Just as it takes time for yeast to make bread rise and good wine to age, taking your time to find that special person and following the proper steps will make your chances for success in a relationship soar. The solution is to find a good friend first.

All long-lasting romantic relationships must have their foundation built on friendship, loving another person as a friend rather than focusing on "being in love." Then, and only then, can you both decide (regardless if you're age fifty, sixty, even seventy plus) how you want this relationship to go. Do you want to . . .

- Make the relationship permanent through marriage?
- Live together as lovers?
- Live apart and still be lovers?
- Remain single, but enhance your life with a best friend?
- Rethink or reconnect with your orientation and experiment with a lesbian or gay lifestyle?
- Experiment with an "alternative" style that could include a third person with an established couple, or something more unusual?

Too often people jump into this decision state without first shoring up the foundation of their relationship with a strong and lasting friendship. When things move too fast, both men and women often begin to feel challenged as the expectations change and are different. They often avoid commitment because they're not ready to lose what they consider their independence, or they're afraid of being disappointed—again.

In their book, *Life's Big Questions* (Indianapolis, Ind.: Alpha Books, 2002), Presbyterian minister William R. Grimbol and Rabbi Jeffrey R. Astrachan urge us to improve our skills as loving human beings. They write: "Though our American culture has hundreds of books on how to become better sexual lovers, it has few on the subject of how to improve our loving. Many of us may know many exciting positions to enhance our sexual love-making, but few of us know many ways to become more spiritually gifted at loving."

Perfection in Humans Is Imperfect

Disappointment in love—often several times in our lifetime—is a reality in the lives of most people. Love and intimacy are what people seek more than anything else. Yet it is in this realm where most misunderstanding, tragedy, hostility, and confusion occur. False perceptions and unrealistic expectations about the role of love in selecting a partner are the principle reasons why the majority of marriages and other relationships fail miserably. In addition to dispelling some common myths, such as "You really fall in love only once," "Love is blind," "Love is at first sight," and "Sexual satisfaction is synonymous with love," considering the role of love becomes a compelling issue for you to contemplate.

On September 18, 2000, Kathleen Kelleher wrote in *The Los Angeles Times:* "The chance of a first marriage ending in divorce over a forty-year period is 67 percent. Half of all divorces occur in the first seven years of marriage." We're sure it needn't surprise you to learn that the majority of second marriages don't last either. It may be due to false expectations, pressures exerted by family and adult children and stepchildren, or by unresolved differences in values.

A relationship isn't an easy thing to pull off successfully. So don't despair if it doesn't work out. The pressures put on us by our culture are enormous. How many of us have been deluded into thinking that feeling we're in love is enough for a successful relationship? Ads, TV sitcoms, and even respected dramatic shows, for example, recklessly idealize "passion" as being central to a love relationship. But the reality of authentic partnerships more often stems from acts of love including sharing values, respect, open communication, and honesty.

When You Want Something More

If you've had awful love experiences, or have never been in love, or your loving partner is deceased, then this book is for you. Our guess is that you are smart, may still work full-time, have friends, hobbies, or special talents. Yet, even though you may be living well as a single person, it's possible that you aren't as happy as you'd like to be. *Another Chance for Love* is for people who feel as though something or someone is missing from their lives; it's about finding the partner that's right for you, because many people fall in love with people who are absolutely wrong for them.

What *does* matter is the active pursuit of closeness to another person and making the effort to enrich your life through self-development. *Another Chance for Love* is about finding your way to a best friend first, which may then evolve into a love relationship, marriage, or a committed friendship.

You may be one of the 35 million single adults over age forty plus in America who is searching for a committed relationship. If so, you've probably noticed that almost everyone is cautious. The one skill so many of us seem to have mastered is how to end a relationship. We have learned to recognize what we don't want, and we have become experts in saying "good-bye." Take your time; follow the steps in cultivating a relationship you'll read in this book, and then you'll find success.

We encourage you to think about what you *do* want. One of our society's mistakes is that we have inadvertently exaggerated the importance of sex and of finding a so-called "soul mate." We have become confused by unrealistic expectations about what love is supposed to do for us.

We are making the case for passionate friendship as the key ingredient to a fulfilling relationship—not love alone, or "chemistry." Ultimately, liking a person is a prerequisite for loving a person. In any case, love is not enough. Although love can be marvelous and exciting, it's also often so crazy, irrational, and volatile that you can't count on it to last. Love promises intimacy; friendship delivers it.

Open the Door to Friendship

It is a momentous time in our lives when we invite someone else to enter our world, giving it new life and meaning. It is a time loaded with potential. How it turns out will depend in large part on knowing yourself, learning how to like, then love another, and by living in mutuality with your partner. The give-and-take of relationships is liberating, self-fulfilling, and sometimes self-sacrificing. It gives us joy to be part of another's life, even in times of sadness.

While it's true that to have a friend you have to be one, it's also true that to develop a caring relationship with someone, you have to first open the door to friendship. According to author C. S. Lewis: "Friendship is born at the moment when one person says to another, 'What! You, too? I thought I was the only one.'"

This book will help lead you to that special moment.

Chapter 1

What Do
You Want?

"Young love is a flame; very pretty, often very hot and fierce, but still only light and flickering. The love of the older and disciplined heart is as coals, deep-burning, unquenchable."

—Henry Ward Beecher (1813–1887),
American clergyman

FREUD IS CREDITED with saying, "Women! What do they want?" But the same could be said for men. Trying to verbalize just what it is you want in a new relationship is somewhat like trying to describe a fluffy cloud moving slowly across the sky; it keeps changing form. One reason verbalizing what you want is so hard is that you really don't know, not exactly.

A widow of one year tried to explain it. "I don't want to date . . . not yet anyway. But I miss having someone to talk to. I have women friends, but . . . Well, maybe I'd like just to have a companion—a man—to have dinner with or go to the theater with . . . but with nothing more expected." She faltered. "I really don't know *what* I want."

It's not easy. It's not that you're lonely, not really. You do have a lot of friends, but—and there's that "but" again—what you may be struggling with is that you want a friend, a special friend, to call when something good happens, or something sad, or when you really need a hug or a pat on the back. You're

1

looking for someone whose company you enjoy and perhaps it will develop into a long-term or permanent relationship. But not necessarily or necessary.

Clarify Your Thoughts

First you need to back up and consider what you want in a relationship. Actually get a tablet or notebook and write down your thoughts or use your computer to type them out. Writing them down, rather than just idly thinking about what you want, makes them real and helps to clarify your thoughts. Think about questions such as these:

- Do you want someone who shares your interests such as a love for ballet, movies, theater, music, cooking, football, or travel? Could you be happy with someone who doesn't share your interests?
- Is good sex the most important part of a relationship for you? What if you found someone who was perfect in every other way, but who was unable to have sex? Are you a sensual person who craves cuddling and caressing? How important is it for you to find someone who enjoys giving and receiving those touches?
- What are your values? Would you write off someone who didn't share them? Which ones are absolute?
- How important are good looks? If you're a man, would you write off an otherwise "perfect" woman because she was taller than you? What if she were plain, overweight, or older? If you're a woman and you've found an otherwise "ideal" man, would you reject him because he's younger than you? Fat or bald? Do you want a "trophy" partner, someone who looks good and makes you feel more important because he or she is on your arm?

- Is money—too much or too little—a consideration for you in forming a relationship?
- Do you feel you have to have a man (or woman) in your life to feel complete?
- Do your personalities need to mesh? What are you really like as a person? Be honest. Are you shy and introverted, enjoying nothing more than a fine dinner and a good book to read by the fire, or are you someone who must always be on the go—dancing, traveling, involved in the world around you? What if the otherwise perfect person is your personality opposite?
- What are your responsibilities? Do you have teenage or adult children? Grandchildren? Aging parents or other relatives you're responsible for? How would someone new fit into your time and emotional commitments?
- What are your quirks? Are you a compulsive cleaner with no clutter and a model-house look in your home? Are you comfortable with dirty laundry in a pile on the floor and stacks of papers lying on tables, chairs, and the floor? Are you into exercise? Meditation? Does the new person in your life need to conform or are you comfortable with differences?
- What are your dreams of "someday"? How would someone new fit into these dreams?
- How do you feel about religious, ethnic, or racial differences?

There is a quiz at the end of this chapter to help you determine the significance to the answers to these and other questions.

Build Bridges, Not Walls

We agree with the words of Joseph Fort Newton, an American clergyman, who wrote, "People are lonely because they build walls instead of bridges." And it's so true. We often are not even aware that we're doing so, but there we are, going right ahead piling rejection brick up on rejection brick and then wondering why we can't find anyone through the wall we've built. It's not that "all men are either married or gay" or that "women don't want men anymore." It's that we've stacked our wall of standards so high that no mortal could fill the position. Sadly, it's possible that the person who would perfectly fill our needs is standing on the other side of the wall we've built.

You may be unconsciously creating obstacles to finding a satisfying relationship by rejecting someone before you really get to know him or her first as a friend. That's why before you can reach out to someone else, you need to understand who you are and what you want out of life.

Focus on Friendship First

To determine what it is you really want in a relationship, begin to focus only on the friendship aspect of a relationship, not on whether or not you're in love or could love this person. Unlike the myth of "love at first sight," most mature love grows as it is gently nurtured, rather than hitting you on the head with cupid's bow.

When you're looking for someone special, and you're not satisfied with your present lifestyle, don't look for love or sex; focus on friendships. You'll find a great deal more about why you should focus on friendships first in Chapter 2.

"Dear Abby," now written by Jeanne Phillips, daughter of Abigail Van Buren, echoed these thoughts as she responded to the question: "Can two people who have been friends for a long time become lovers and make it work?" She answered: "Friendship can be a great base for a romantic relationship. Lack of a solid friendship is often the reason that infatuation fails."

I (Sol) have often felt that my greatest achievements in life have been the friends I've made, far more important than my professional accomplishments—especially since I always felt that my late wife, Judith, blessed is her memory, was my best friend.

After forty-two years of marriage, I (Elaine) point to my husband, known as "Hinks," as my best friend. When something good happens to me, I don't consider it has happened until I've shared it with Hinks. When there's sadness or disappointment, as there is in everyone's life, he is there to comfort me. When I was diagnosed with breast cancer, his arms supported me and gave me strength.

So where do you find friends like this? You can't buy them on eBay or order them through the Internet and they certainly don't pop up out of cakes. You have to meet people, develop a friendship, and then see what grows, but all this takes time, a commodity most of us find in short supply. You'll find more specifics on how and where to find potential special friendships in Chapter 6.

A Good Friend Is Hard to Find

Authentic friendships are hard to come by these days. In a nationwide Gallup poll, nearly half the respondents complained that either they do not have time for their friends or they want closer relationships with the friends they have. Certainly, friendship has become the most neglected relationship of our busy and anxious times. "Friendship" is a rather ordinary word, but it carries extraordinary significance in our lives. We hear about friendship so often that it's easy to take those friendships we do have for granted. And most people do, to their everlasting regret.

Like most things that are worthwhile in life, however, real friendship isn't given to us unchallenged and free of obstacles.

You need to share knowledge of yourself and have empathy to help a friend through difficult times. You'll want to find this quality in friends as well, a friend who opens up to you, trusting you to keep confidences and offer support and empathy. Studies confirm that women tend to find it easier to share "intimate" information with their friends than men, who have been conditioned since boyhood to "tough it out" and "suck it up." "Real men," they were taught as toddlers, don't cry, and many men still adhere to this aging myth. But men do cry, and should, for their own mental health and well-being.

You also want a friend who knows how to respond to difficult, problematic circumstances you're facing, but, as Ralph Waldo Emerson is often quoted: "The only way to have a friend is to be one."

A critical aspect of friendship is not to respond to problems in a glib manner. One of the serious barriers to helping a friend in trouble might be called the know-it-all factor. Know-it-alls seem to have all the answers to our problems. If it involves a crisis in our family, for example, they tell us what we should do rather than listening as we sort out our options. In the case of our grief over the loss of a loved one, they offer clichés such as "Time heals, get on with your life" or "You should think of dating again." Easy to say—but far too easy to be of any help to a friend in trouble. "The challenge," as noted family therapist Virginia Satir once said, "is how to give feedback so it comes as a gift rather than criticism."

Look for friends who can feel another's sentiments and keep a tight rein on all advice and judgments. Sometimes, just being with a friend and listening is the best help a friend can give. Remember, though, that while you need someone who can feel this empathy, you also need to be sure that you have acquired this skill in return.

Traits to Consider in a Good Friend

In addition to empathy, there are other qualities that should be important to you as you meet new friends. Weigh them carefully as they can impact your life, especially if a friendship relationship develops into something more permanent.

Similar Value Systems

Partners can have different interests. In fact, different interests make for a stronger relationship. On the other hand, don't expect a relationship to grow or last if you and your partner differ greatly when it comes to personal values. It helps, too, if partners share ethical and/or spiritual goals. This doesn't necessarily mean sharing the same religious beliefs, but a common spirituality and acceptance of the other's religious doctrine. A feeling of common destiny and a strong sense of loyalty should pervade the relationship.

This doesn't mean that you both need to love dressing up for black tie functions, enjoy fine wines, or get a kick out of buying something at a bargain price. It goes far deeper into what is truly important to you. It's the difference between your returning a dollar because you received too much change and your prospective partner bragging that he or she hasn't paid income tax for two years. It's abiding by the speed limit or speeding when there are no police around. It's your sense of right and wrong, of what's fair, of what's moral.

Trust

Frank Crane, an American clergyman and journalist, said, "You may be deceived if you trust too much, but you will live in torment if you do not trust enough." We can't conceive of a successful relationship in which the parties don't trust one another. Trust allows you to accept what the other person is saying at face value, without wondering or agonizing over whether you can really believe it.

Sometimes you may find it difficult to trust a beginning relationship, especially if you've been burned before. But you need to put the singed sorrows behind you and allow trust to grow. Let your potential partner know early that you feel trust is an important element in any relationship—friendship or romantic. Remember there is an "us" in the middle of trust; trust has to exist for both of you for it to prosper.

Effective Communication Skills

Many people think of communication merely as speaking; but a vital part of communication is listening. Unfortunately, most of us aren't born with good listening skills. These are important qualities we develop with practice. Be concerned if you spend time with someone who avoids controversial issues by saying, "I don't want to talk about it," anytime a conflict or disagreement arises. Differences don't go away. They don't even have to be agreed upon as long as each person feels he or she has been heard. Chapter 10 deals with important ways to strengthen your communication skills.

Carol, a middle-age woman who has been married for more than forty years, admits that, in the beginning of her marriage, it was difficult for her to talk about feelings. "I'd either shut down or cry, neither of which helped at all. My husband, however, was patient and helped me to express how I felt. Open communication is now an important part of the success of our marriage. There's nothing we can't and don't talk about."

Intimacy is the closeness, and trust is the gift that comes after making an effort to communicate effectively with a partner.

Trust is the result of honest and open communication so you don't waste valuable time wondering whether or not to really believe what you've just heard. It's a major indicator of our ability to sustain a caring, loving relationship through good times and bad.

A Sense of Humor

Look for someone with a good sense of humor and be willing to laugh at yourself and at the world at large as well. If a person can find humor in a situation, especially one that is troublesome or sad, you've probably met someone worth knowing who is a pleasure to be with. This trait is so attractive that it often makes up for what is lacking in other areas. Laughter reduces blood pressure, tension, and improves blood circulation. It reduces stress and lifts the weight of depression. If you've found someone who enjoys laughter—not at another's expense, but just at the craziness of life—you've found a treasure.

Attitude on Equality

Your success in a relationship increases enormously when both partners have an understanding of the importance respect plays in that relationship—respect for each other as individuals with an equal responsibility to make the relationship work as well as the ability to enjoy equal benefits from that relationship. That sense of respect for one another as equal partners must carry over to a willingness to share responsibility in career, leisure, care for elderly parents and relatives, as well as lifestyle choices. This means sharing the work load without labeling some work as "women's work" and others as "men's work," a concept that may seem strange at first if that isn't the way chores were handled in the past. But trust us; it works better that way.

Responsible Attitude About Money

Take the time to carefully explore each other's attitude about financial matters before your relationship deepens into a romance. If one of you believes in paying cash for everything while the other blesses credit cards, or one is a gambler while the other a saver, you may be headed for problems somewhere down the line. Experts say differences in attitudes toward money and not religious differences are the major reason for breakups in marriage and relationships in general.

Willingness to Share Experiences

A relationship grows over time, filled with a repository of mutual undertakings, private conversations, quiet intimacies, rituals, and traditions you both now share. In many cases, the rituals and traditions are not specifically the ones you grew up with, but a merged version bringing in the best or most meaningful of both, reflecting what is special to each of you. Create your special days—the day you met, your first date, and so on. Take turns making a special meal, write a poem, or draw a greeting card with your personal message.

Loyalty

Loyalty in any type of a personal relationship is a vital element and, indeed, must be the foundation on which that relationship is built in order to let individuals know where they stand and that neither will be undermined in any way by the other. We all have been in social situations where one individual puts down or openly criticizes his or her partner even if it's done in a somewhat joking manner. It's not only embarrassing for bystanders, but it also makes one wonder what the private relationship must be if there is so little loyalty in public. That form of disloyalty weakens a relationship.

Loyalty includes a commitment to each other's growth in career, talents, and sense of purpose or cause. It doesn't necessarily mean that you need to take up that cause as your own, however. You both are still individuals, even as you move toward becoming partners.

Respect for Each Other's Feelings and Wishes

Respect for each other's feelings and wishes is also a form of empathy and honest communication. It is shown by the willingness to delay one's own short-term desires in the knowledge that similar willingness will exist on the part of the other person at a later time. It includes, but is not limited to, respect for the partner's feelings toward sex in any given instance as well as the need to have some time alone.

Respect also is needed for each other's choice of friends and different leisure time interests. Contrary to what many people think, individuals who use jealousy to get their own way at the detriment of their partner are displaying disrespect, not love.

Passion

"Aha," you say. "I knew it would come down to sex." But you're wrong. Passion does not mean just a healthy, robust sex life, although we recommend that aspect as well. Many people in lasting relationships have spoken to us about how they delight in their partner's "passion" for golf or tennis or "passion" for art or classical music. You don't need to share that passion, but just enjoy seeing your partner caught up in it. Sometimes that passion is catching and you, too, will expand and explore those interests.

Charles is married to a woman who has been an ardent Tampa Bay Buccaneer fan since 1976, when the Tampa Bay area received the franchise. "At first, I went along to the games because she loved them so," he admitted. "I knew very little about football as I'm really not much into team sports. Sailing's my passion. The team had so many problems for so long, it was hard to stay interested. But I adored her for staying true to her love of the Bucs. Little by little, I began to understand the plays, recognized penalties before they were announced, and knew the players by name. January 2003, we watched as our team won the Super Bowl. I was as excited as my wife was. I was enveloped by the same passion as she was. It's one more thing we now share in our lives . . . and yes, she's become an ardent sailor, too."

Attitude Toward Sharing in Domestic Duties

Talk about how each of you feels about household tasks before spending time at the other's home or actually living together. It's important to accept responsibility for doing a fair share of the more unpleasant household or family tasks and not to be limited by gender stereotypes. Ellen's husband takes the dry cleaning to the laundry and often does the grocery shopping while Ellen changes lightbulbs and takes care of minor home repairs and arranges for major ones. She cooks, he clears, and she puts the dishes in the dishwasher. They make their king-size bed together. "We never really discussed who would do what," she mused. "We just sort of volunteered for the parts we liked best."

It can weaken a relationship when one partner takes on a martyr role, claiming a monopoly on all the household tasks. Often, however, women have only themselves to blame for being overwhelmed with household chores because they criticize the male's efforts to the point that he says: "Okay. Then *you* do it." If you're a woman, ask yourself: "Does it just need to be done or be done perfectly?"

Seven Guidelines

While these points should give you an idea of what you want in a relationship, they aren't the only ones you might consider. Psychologist Albert Ellis lists seven guidelines in *Making Intimate Connections* (Atascadero, Calif.: Impact Publications, 2000) by Albert Ellis and Ted Crawford. They include:

1. Accept your partner "as is."
2. Express appreciation frequently.
3. Communicate with integrity.
4. Share and explore differences with your partner.
5. Support your partner's goals.
6. Give your partner the right to be wrong.
7. Reconsider your wants as goals.

Questions to Ponder

In addition to Dr. Ellis's guidelines, there are other questions to ask yourself and then to answer honestly:

- Am I willing to take the risk of opening myself up to another person in order to get to know a new friend, recognizing that it may not develop into something special?
- Am I comfortable with myself as I am or do I feel I need to "act the part" in order to be noticed, seem interesting, or feel more comfortable when I meet others for the first time?

- If I've met someone, do I like myself more in the presence of this person—or less? Is my self-esteem enhanced or do I feel anxious that I might do something dumb or otherwise screw up before he or she gets to really know me?
- Have I considered what type of arrangement is best for me? In discovering my own voice, am I okay if I decide I want to remain single but in a nonmarital partnership, become part of a nonsexual companionship, or enter into a gay or lesbian relationship?
- Do I feel there's a deadline hanging over my head or am I willing to take the time required to let a friendship develop first? Do I feel I'm getting too old to find somebody and I'll "settle"?
- Am I realistic about my expectations of what I have to bring into a new relationship? Of what I might expect from a new relationship?
- Do I fall for a partner's energy and clever patter before determining whether that partner can also be a caring and responsible person?
- Do I equate jealousy with love?
- Do I feel good about myself just as I am or do I need affirmation from others in order to feel valued?
- Do I allow ghosts of the past to haunt me and spook new relationships? If I've had previous breakups, have I examined them to try to determine the reasons for the breakup, learning from them so I don't make the same mistakes again?
- Do I have confidence in myself and have the strength to be accountable to myself or do I need input from my family and friends to advise me what I should do (and who I should do it with)?
- Am I kind to others, especially those who serve me, such

as wait staff and sales clerks? Do I observe how a potential partner treats others?

- Do I know my potential partner well enough and like him or her enough to work through periods of disappointment and unmet expectations regarding love and sex?
- Do I feel committed to working out our differences?
- What are my core values and are any of them negotiable?

Don't just read through these questions hurriedly. Take your time. You may want to return to them a few times to consider how you really feel. Be honest. After all, no one else is going to see your answers. After you've thought about your answers to these questions, then you can move along the road to finding your best friend and, perhaps, a lifetime companion.

Chapter 2

Why Put Friendship First?

"If we would build on a sure foundation in friendship,
we must love friends for their sake rather than for our own."

—Charlotte Brontë (1816–1855), English writer

PUTTING FRIENDSHIP FIRST is such an important concept, and so integral to the message of this book, that we decided to devote an entire chapter to it. Friendships have always added significantly to our lives and have done so since we first were toddlers meeting a stranger in nursery school and discovering that we both liked to build tunnels in the sandbox. But friendships become especially valuable as we grow older. Why? It's not because it's easier to find friends than lovers (although that may often be true), but rather that friends can give us what we need most at this period of our lives—nonjudgmental emotional support, companionship, trust, shared values, a humorous outlook on life, and respect, to mention a few.

Ah, you may think. Aren't these the same traits we look for in a special partner, a companion in life? Yes, but with the caveat that in friendship, there must be a sense of equality, a quality often sadly lacking in many intimate relationships. As far back as the 1700s, Françoise d'Aubigne Maintenon, consort of Louis XIV, summed it up by saying, "There is an important difference between love and friendship. While the former delights in extremes and opposites, the latter demands equality."

17

Why We're Easier on Our Friends

We're much kinder to friends and don't judge them in as harsh a light as we do potential partners and, as you'll read in the next chapter, the media doesn't blind us with a myriad of images of what we all should desire as the "perfect" friend. That leaves us to follow our instincts, striking up friendships where we find them, ever expanding our social circle with regulars we see at the grocery, the gym, our church or synagogue activities and services, at charity auctions, art gallery openings, and through other friends and acquaintances.

Judy, a forty-three-year-old divorced woman from Missouri, says: "I just do what I enjoy doing and meet men in the process. That way you automatically know you have one thing in common. For example, I play ultimate Frisbee, so I meet men on the field. I also do this old-fashioned form of dance called "contra dancing," which is a wonderful way to meet men and actually get physical, friendly, nonpredatory touch. I meet people at the gym, too. I thought my friends would set me up, but so far no one has even suggested it. That's fine, but amusing, given that I thought they'd jump at the chance."

We tend to be more open-minded when it comes to "imperfections" in our friends, even when they don't quite match up to our mental list of what we require or even prefer in a date or potential partner. It doesn't matter if our friends are taller or shorter, younger or older, rather plain, a little too heavy, bald, or of a different race, religion, or ethnic background than we are, or any of the other endless list of potential dis-qualifiers we use when dating. For most of us, racial, ethnic, and religious differences among our friends just make them that more interesting and not really a concern even as the friendship progresses.

Sally, a fifty-nine-year-old woman, summed it up nicely by

saying: "I was single in my early thirties and forties and again in my mid-fifties. The first time it was from being divorced, and the second time, I was widowed. For any significant relationship of more than just a few dates, I have always known the guy for a while, primarily having met him at work or outside activity—a singing group and backstage acquaintances or shopping for antiques. In most cases, there has been something of a friendship first, as I look back on many different guys over the years. Looks really ain't it. You get involved with someone and those 'just okay' looks suddenly become a lot more than 'okay.' Yup, he has to have appeal, but that can be a far cry from just the right height, hair color, etc."

Why Men and Women Can Be "Just" Friends

Numerous books have been written extolling the value of close friendships between women, which Judith Viorst calls "open and intimate" in her book *Necessary Losses*. Some, but far fewer, have been written about the close friendships between heterosexual men, what we like to call the "business-sports connection," which is approximately the level on which these male buddies converse.

Oddly, the only flashing red light of alarm seems to be triggered by others when a woman begins to develop a platonic friendship with a heterosexual man, especially if he happens to be younger than she. Homosexual men, on the other hand, are considered to be "safe" friends for a woman (that is, they're not interested in having sex).

According to Carol Cassell from the Institute for Sexuality Education and Equity, in Albuquerque, New Mexico, "strong cultural pressures are mounted against the development of such friendships [with heterosexual men]." "But," she stresses, "the advantages to be derived transcend these barriers. These friendships can be the catalyst for breaking down the obstacles of sex-role stereotyping and form a revolutionary way for the sexes to interact." Dr. Cassell adds, in the book, *Human Sexuality*, an encyclopedia edited by Vera L. Bullough and Bonnie Bullough, "undoubtedly, men and women who are unabashedly intimate friends—platonic or erotic—will shake up the segregated sex roles of society's 'old order' by calling for a permanent truce in the battle of the sexes. Female-male friendship is a concept whose time has come."

In her book, *The Unofficial Guide to Dating Again*, author Tina B. Tessina, Ph.D., M.F.T., suggests you think in terms of the "un-date," a term she has used to denote casually getting together "without the commitment and interest implied by an actual date." This type of a meeting relieves you of any worry of "Does he think I'm interested?" or "Is she going to expect me to ask her out?" It is simply two friends having coffee together, going to the opening of a new art gallery, or just sitting in the park, listening to band music. "Un-date" is a great term to think about and to put into your vocabulary as you make new friends.

Jerome, a divorced fifty-year-old, says: "At my 'advanced' age, I definitely want to be friends first. I am in this for the long haul and having sex too early in a relationship is likely to muck things up as I think it clouds everyone's judgment and makes it harder to withdraw gracefully if it isn't the right match. And though passion and sex are very important to me, having a strong friendship with my partner/spouse is at least just as important to me. I have met a number of potential partners who turned out not to be the right match for various reasons, but who have remained friends. I like that."

Friends Are Good for Your Well-Being

Making friends and, perhaps even more important, having a best friend can be a crucial factor in strengthening your self-esteem, a trait that may be a little shaky or totally absent after you've done battle with either being divorced, being widowed, or just experiencing too many years of not finding the lifetime companion of whom most of us have dreamed or at least anticipated as our just due. Feeling good about yourself is more than just a clever catch phrase found in most self-help books; it actually becomes an energy force for you. When your self-esteem is boosted, you become more optimistic, you treat the people around you with kindness, and yes, you smile a lot. And when you smile, others smile back at you.

It's not a new thought. Samuel Pepys wrote in his diary on October 31, 1662: "As happy a man as any in the world, for the whole world seems to smile upon me." Focusing on positive feelings makes your world look hopeful and makes you look much more appealing to the world. A good friend helps generate such feelings within you. What a blessing it is to have friends.

Good Friendships Need Nurturing

It's unfortunate that authentic friendships are harder to come by these days. Perhaps our time is too filled with one-minute everything, e-mail, faxes, voice mail, and call waiting. We're communicating through machines where empathy and emotion don't compute. Indeed, friendship has become the most neglected relationship of our busy and anxious times. It is a loss, because often these friendships might be the seed of what could grow into the permanent special relationship you covet.

Never minimize the importance that friendships play in your life; they are extremely important. Even if none of your close friendships ever develop into a permanent relationship, how lucky you are to have good friends in your life. Often, some of these opposite-gender friends may stay friends even after you've found a partner. Our friends enrich our lives—and it really doesn't matter if they are male or female, gay or straight, young or old.

Connie, a divorced single mother, who moved from the New York area to Colorado, can vouch for the truth in the importance of friends. For her, one good friend soon became three. "I started hiking with a group called Boulder Singles Hike, hoping that I might meet someone special through that group," she said. "I dated a couple of men I met that way a few times, but my greatest treasure was John, a man who has become one of my closest friends—and who now lives with my neighbor, Val, also a dear friend, who was widowed when she was in her early forties.

"John has always had women pals and I've always had men pals and the two of us like to go hiking or cross-country skiing together. Fortunately, Val isn't the least bit jealous or possessive of John. I don't believe that either John or I ever thought about a more intimate physical relationship. I know I didn't, because I treasure true friendships and don't like to mess them up with intimacy that might backfire.

"Just before John and Val began seeing each other, I, through a complicated combination of mutual friends and circumstances, met the man to whom I'm now married. We'll celebrate our tenth anniversary this September. My husband also is not jealous, angry, or upset when I go mountain climbing with John, which, as far as I'm concerned, is just another of his fine qualities. We live two houses apart from John and Val and we remain good friends."

Judy, whom you met at the beginning of this chapter, found that even a relationship you've decided you don't want to blossom into romance can still remain as a good friendship. "I spend time with one man who has two kids," she said. "We remain 'just friends' because I don't like the way he parents them."

You Have to Work to Sustain a Good Friendship

Good friendships don't just happen—and they don't sail along on constant smooth waters either. Often, there's turbulence and a struggle to know exactly what to say or not say to help a friend through difficult times, such as a divorce, death of a partner, loss of a job, an unwanted breakup, or unpleasantness with a grown child. While some people have the gift to do the right things instinctively, most of us labor as we strive to do our best. Our friends value this effort, just as we do theirs when we are troubled or in pain and they have to improvise to figure out how they best can be of comfort.

Often, it is this test of friendship by fire that jolts us into realizing the power of a particular friendship. It underscores the intimacy that is the foundation of any strong relationship, be it friendship, partnership, or marriage. It implies a sense of safety, trust, and respect, especially respect for confidences told from the heart. Marlene Dietrich is often quoted for saying: "It is the friends that you can call at four A.M. that matter." How true. Is it worthwhile to go through all this in order to maintain a friendship? Absolutely.

Intimacy in Platonic Friendships

In the February 1997 issue of *The New Woman,* Harriet Lerner wrote: "An intimate relationship is one in which we can be who we are (rather than what the other person wants and expects us to be) and allow the person to do the same. This means we can say what we think and feel in a relatively uncensored way, and we can share both our competence and our vulnerability without having to hide or exaggerate either . . . An intimate relationship enlarges—rather than diminishes—our sense of the world and ourselves."

It is this very sense of emotional intimacy that must be the basis of a good friendship and the foundation of any physical relationship that may develop into a more permanent relationship. If you don't have this sense of trust and complete respect with a friend, it certainly won't magically develop if you decide to become partners.

Vivian learned this shortly after she was divorced. "Jim came into my life shortly after my divorce so I knew I was still 'desirable.' Yes, believe it or not, that's a feeling I experienced after finding myself 'alone' after a thirty-six-year marriage. He provided me with the physical touch I yearned for after a long drought and some days of fun and laughter. I knew that it was the first relationship after my divorce and served as a reflection of who I am and can be, and that it was not the love of my life. Just the love of the moment.

"But Jim felt guilty about his divorce, feeling that he had failed in his marriage. He was intent on making it up to his kids by doting on them, plying them with gifts and electronic toys, chauffeuring them everywhere, attending *every* hockey game in which all three kids were involved. So I knew he had a priority list. His kids first, his work second, time for himself to recharge and zone out with his drinking buddies or fishing, and lastly, me.

"Time for me meant e-mailing me mostly. Phone calls might come on occasion, on his way to or from driving his kids to school, to see if I was available for a half-hour visit. After not hearing from him for days, he'd call late at night, probably after a drink or two, and ask if I could come to his house for the night. In the year that we were seeing each other (during which he constantly fretted about the age difference and even asked me to color the natural white streak in my hair), he took me out to dinner only once, to an inexpensive Mexican restaurant. He much preferred coming to my house, where I prepared candlelit dinners, the caliber of which blew his socks off. He never once took me to a movie.

"I now am in a relationship where I am accepted for who I am. He is self-assured and assures me of my beauty, positiveness, and more. He thinks the white streak in my hair is sexy! There is reciprocity in this relationship, something that wasn't present in my relationship with Jim."

Vivian's experiences only emphasize the importance of what she calls "reciprocity" and what we call "mutual respect, trust, and intimacy." Intimacy is greatly enhanced by what the psychotherapist David Schnarch calls "differentiation," which is based on the assumption of the uniqueness of each human being. In his book, *Passionate Marriage*, Schnarch writes, "The more differentiated we are—the stronger our sense of self-definition and the better we can hold ourselves together during conflicts with our partners—the more intimacy we can tolerate with someone we love without fear of losing our sense of who we are as separate beings."

Becoming a Friendship Stowaway

Although our friendships—either same gender or opposite gender—are important in our lives, they sometimes also can become a safe hiding place. It's often easier for a woman to ask a male friend—either gay or straight (but not interested in a physical relationship)—to serve as an escort to a function, or for a single male to go stag, rather than to take the risk of asking someone who could become more than just a friend, and thus offering some possibility of a future serious relationship.

Women also often opt for the less scary way out by going to the movies or theater, dinner, or traveling with their female friends rather than taking the risk of asking a man who might say no, although he also could say yes. According to Helena Hacker Rosenberg, in her book, *How to Get Married After 35*, "women who move in packs such as these put themselves at a decided social disadvantage because no man wants to run a gauntlet of females to strike up a chat with one of them." It's not a lot different than the boys at your junior high dances who stood on one side of the dance floor pretending not to notice the girls on the other side, who were giggling and looking formidable. It took a brave youngster to cross the line—and even in middle and middle-old age, many men still can't make that bold move.

Does this mean that you can't enjoy the company of your women friends, with whom you feel at ease? Of course not. But it does suggest that you also consider occasionally going on the offense by asking the men you've already become friendly with to share a dinner or movie with you, taking a day cruise to nowhere, or (horrors of horrors) going solo to the opening of a new art gallery, practicing putting at a golf course, or signing up (alone) for Spanish class. You might not meet the man of your dreams, but you may make a new friend.

Focus on friendship first. It doesn't matter what you call this relationship—*amigo* (*amiga*), companion, pal, best friend, bosom buddy, or just plain buddy—as long as you develop one or more. As rich as the English language is, it really doesn't have one word that specifically expresses a close friendship with someone, which is too bad because friendship is so important. It's a lot like learning how to dance the tango. It's great to know the steps, but until you have a partner, you're really not dancing.

Get to know the steps for friendship first. Feel comfortable with the other person. You may feel a little vulnerable at first. You will, actually. But as you open up and communicate honestly, respecting one another's opinions even though you may not agree with them and appreciating each other's differences, you'll begin to relax and just enjoy the flow of friendship. If it happens that both of your feelings grow, it may be time to show each other you care. Move into the physical side of your relationship only when you both feel ready.

Keep communication lines open. No games between partners. There has to be a sense of trust. Then, hopefully, you will realize that by maintaining a friendship first and foremost, you are ready to become true partners and share your lives, remaining friends in every sense of the word.

Chapter 3

Getting to
Know Yourself

"We're running on different tracks.
Your work takes you into cities;
I'm a cave dweller at heart.
We're chasing different foxes.
Yours is exciting, star-spangled;
Mine, tame and plain.
We're climbing different mountains.
Yours is snow-covered, dark with danger;
Mine is safe and flower-filled.
But I know you,
And you know me,
And we have our meeting place."

—Elaine Fantle Shimberg

ALTHOUGH WE'VE BEEN in our own skins for many years, many of us haven't taken the time to really get to know ourselves. Instead, we seem content to identify ourselves by the perceptions of others, singing their songs rather than discovering the rhythm of our own lives. That may be one of the reasons so many middle-age and older people still seek the special friend, a lifetime companion, a lover.

Find Your Own Voice

Finding your own voice means being open to new ideas and experiences. It means not remaining victimized by previous traumatic or agonizing events. It means being hopeful about the possibility of change and not being focused on or comparing yourself with others. It's vital for your happiness to find your own voice—*your* voice, and not echoes of the voices you still hear from your parents or friends about who you are or what is right or wrong for you. Do you think you're too old to change? You're not.

Your Perceptions Become Your Reality

Unfortunately, what we think often becomes our reality—good or bad. If we think we're unlovable, we send off similar vibes, sending people scurrying away. People who appear insecure and desperate or who engage in sex too early in the relationship often send unattractive signals. People who place too much emphasis on their wealth or on "ego trips" also give off negative vibes.

Michael S. Broder, author of *The Art of Living Single*, suggests that the difficulty in finding someone can be the fear of being hurt or rejected, which often stems from a history of being abused. At the core can be low self-esteem. Low self-esteem can develop when you focus on all the bad things that have happened to you, such as divorce or death of a spouse, and think all these events were your fault. You take ownership of everything, from a loved one dying of a heart attack—"Why didn't I get him to the hospital sooner? Why didn't I recognize his symptoms"—to a broken relationship because the partner was abusive, alcoholic, bipolar, and so on. How powerful you must be to have controlled all these events. The truth is, of course, that you didn't cause them. You were just part of the fallout.

The problem with stewing about things you could not have caused is that it can lead to depression, an overwhelming sadness causing fatigue, loss of appetite, difficulty sleeping or sleeping too much, and a pervading sense of hopelessness. If you find yourself suffering from these symptoms, you should seek counseling by a qualified therapist. Chapter 4 will tell you more about depression and give you some ideas of what to do when you're feeling stuck.

There Is a Power in Positive Thinking

There's a reason why Norman Vincent Peale's book, *The Power of Positive Thinking,* is still widely read even after its original publication in 1952. Because it works. And many others have lauded positive thinking as well. Henry Thoreau said: "Men [that is, people] are born to succeed, not fail." Ralph Waldo Emerson said the same thing when he wrote: "Self-trust is the first secret of success." Norman Vincent Peale wrote in his book, *You Can If You Think You Can,* "you can if you think you can. Engrave those seven words deeply in consciousness. They are packed with power and with truth."

Why waste time thinking, "I'll never meet anybody special. Nobody would want me at this point in my life. I'm too old [short, fat, bald, whatever]," when instead you could tell yourself, "I like myself. I'm fun to be with and a caring person. I can find lots of new friends to enjoy." Once you say that often enough, you'll start believing it yourself. You'll smile more, lose that "needy" look, and forget yourself because you're learning to enjoy others. That's makes you more interesting to people who are somewhat less than perfect, just as we all are.

Be sure to be honest as you list your attributes. Are you

really a good listener, for example, or do you interrupt frequently? Listening is a vital part of good communication skills. Consider compliments you have received. Have you just sloughed them off, thinking, "They don't know what they're talking about?" But maybe they really do. So when someone says, "You have such a knack for decorating," or "It makes me feel good just talking to you," practice saying a simple "thank-you" and jot that positive trait down on your list.

Make a list of your strong points. Forget the fact that your waist is bigger than it was in college or that your hair is getting thin and you aren't. Focus on your abilities and personal qualities. Are you thoughtful toward others? A good cook? Do you like animals? Children? Do you have a good sense of humor? Are you creative? Can you fix leaky faucets, computers, or VCRs? Take time to write down as many good points as you can think of. Tape the sheet to your bathroom mirror and read your list each morning and before you go to bed. Before long, you'll find that you really do believe these positive things about yourself, as you should.

What other faulty perceptions are causing you problems? What are your perceptions about relationships? Friendships? Are these thoughts and myths holding you back? And if you are divorced or have a history of shattered love affairs, have you thought about why this happens to you or have you always considered it to be the other's fault? If you think you may have played a part as well, spend some time figuring out what mistakes you might have made so you can try to handle things differently next time.

Once you find your own voice to change flawed perceptions and accept reality, you become strong enough as an individual to increase the possibility of having an intimate, fulfilling, and lasting relationship.

Mother Was Right: Pretty Is As Pretty Does

One way to find your own voice is by achieving intimacy with others through friendship first. Be patient. It is through friendship that the best and most lasting relationships develop. But first you may have to tear down some of the barriers you have set up to protect yourself against rejection and being hurt.

Many people go to psychologists, psychiatrists, social workers, or a member of the clergy to receive help and advice on how to find someone to love them. Often, they are overly concerned with their looks and attribute the absence of a partner in their lives to their unattractiveness. They may be asked to consider the people they know who are in relationships or are married and whether these people are happy. If the answer is in the affirmative, they're asked if these people are necessarily the best-looking people? Often, they are not. In one case, a woman described her best friend as "short and heavy," but said she was "very happily married to a skinny, unattractive guy." She soon realized the point: When two people like and love each other, sexual attraction and intimacy can emerge.

That's why it's so important not to get so hung up on our looks, especially when certain factors such as height cannot be changed. People who hate themselves and express it in acting—not actually looking—unattractive, tend to repel rather than attract others. Believing that certain perfumes, hair tonics, hygienic sprays, Botox injections, or selected sexual techniques will make you attractive gets you nowhere. A person who understands his or her self-worth and who is genuine becomes appealing to others.

For every negative you can think of, a positive example can be found. Here's one example: "Women don't like bald men." Think of Sean Connery, one of the sexiest men alive, according to magazine polls. Here's another: "Men don't like heavy women." Elizabeth Taylor at her heaviest was still a picture of beauty. As your mother often told you: "It's the beauty within that people see."

In their book, *Men Like Women Who Like Themselves*, authors Steven Carter and Julia Sokol make encouraging statements about women, self-respect, and dating that also apply to men. Therefore, you can easily use the words "man" and "himself" in the following quote: "The smartest woman knows that she always wants to be remembered for who she is, not how she looks or what she's wearing. She always checks in with herself before she checks herself out in the mirror and heads out the door."

There's an amazing aspect of talking with so many people over the years. Many of the most attractive people see themselves as being too thin, too fat, having big thighs, being too ugly because of a facial mole or blemish, having a nose too big, lips too small—you name it. It's important to note that self-deception or an unreal conclusion (often influenced by the media) can be a symbolic death sentence for the ego.

Fake It Until You Can Make It

So how can you change the way you feel about yourself? Follow the old AA expression, "Fake it until you make it." You can alter your mode of behavior, even if you don't feel worthy of love, by acting as if you do. Actions change you, and by acting as if you really feel good about yourself, you'll start believing it. Remember the song in Rodgers and Hammerstein's *Anna and the King of Siam* in which Anna said she could "whistle a happy tune" and pretend she wasn't afraid and before she knew it, she no longer was afraid.

Think More about Others and Less about Yourself

Do you remember the often-told story about the person who monopolized the conversation with talk about himself? Finally, as he caught his breath, he said, "Well, enough about me. Let's talk about you. What do you think about me?"

It's easy to become so self-focused that we forget about others, but the less you think about yourself and more about others, you'll change your thinking and, actually, your actions as well. People who care about others are more lovable. If you're finding it difficult to feel lovable in your own skin, then turn your attention to others who need a helping hand—by doing volunteer work, what we call "mitzvah therapy." As you discover the joy of helping others, you'll also find that you've helped yourself to a better self-image.

You Can Make Yourself Happy

Herbert Benson, M.D., author of the bestseller *The Relaxation Response*, describes in his new book, *Break-Out Principle*, that to break prior mental patterns, it often is necessary to quit concentrating on yourself. Dr. Benson suggests that you "dwell instead on what's happening outside your narrow orbit of self-interest." That's quite true. We often agonize about what to wear to a singles' dance where there will be hundreds of other people, none of whom are really focusing on what we have on. (They're focusing on what *they* are wearing.)

Forget that you've always been a little shy when it comes to meeting people. Turn your attention outward and learn about other people's interests, hopes, and dreams. Ask them questions about themselves. They'll consider you a great conversationalist and not realize that *they* are doing most of the talking. Know your strengths and use them. Focus on what you can do and not on what's difficult for you.

The XIV Dalai Lama follows the Buddhist training or Buddha Dharma. He states: "What becomes important in the understanding of this basic teaching is a genuine awareness of one's own potentials and the need to utilize them to their fullest. Seen in this light, every human action becomes significant."

According to the Dalai Lama, "the purpose of life is to be happy. The sense of contentment is a key factor for attaining happiness . . . As a Buddhist I have found that one's own mental attitude is the most influential factor in working toward that goal. In order to change conditions outside ourselves, whether they concern the environment or relations with others, we must first change within ourselves. Inner peace is key. In that state of mind you can face difficulties with calm and reason, while keeping your inner happiness. The Buddhist teachings of love, kindness, and tolerance, the conduct of nonviolence, and the theory that all things are relative, as well as a variety of techniques for calming the mind, are sources of that inner peace."

Don't worry, it isn't necessary to switch religions in order to profit from the philosophy of Buddhism. Start by reading *The Art of Happiness* by the Dalai Lama and Howard C. Cutter. For other ideas, read *Destructive Emotions* by Daniel Goldman. (Please see the Suggested Reading section at the back of the book for publishing information.)

Sex Isn't Another Word for Intimacy

Many people have a lot of sex but suffer from a lack of intimacy. Betty Friedan, in *Fountain of Age,* writes: "Much sexuality, to be sure, has the quality of intimacy. But genital orgasm can and often does occur without intimacy and even as an offense against it."

If you desire sexual stimulation and you have no partner

and no safe access to sex with someone else, the best thing to do is masturbate. Remember how Woody Allen handled it in the movie *Annie Hall*? "Masturbation is sex with the person you love most, who will never turn you down." There's nothing abnormal about masturbation. In this connection, a good book to read is Betty Dodson's *Liberating Masturbation*.

If what we need isn't sex per se, but rather just to be physically touched—some "holding time"—then we can find it with a few close friends. Close friends, even platonic friends, can give us a hug, a pat on the back, and even the hand holding that makes us feel needed and cared for. Intimacy, true intimacy, is a touching of the minds, not only and not necessarily the bodies. Intimacy is the moment when you say to a special friend, "I was just thinking that," or "I was just going to say that same thing." It also is when you sit quietly and listen as a friend pours out fears and problems and you offer no advice, but just tender comfort by your presence alone. Intimacy also is holding that information in strict confidence and not sharing it with others.

If you crave intimacy, but feel that it escapes you, be sure you aren't inadvertently substituting sexual contact for the emotional contact you desire. Perhaps you're frightening away the very people you're trying to connect with because they, too, want the emotional union and tender touches without necessarily always becoming sexual.

Are You Trying Too Hard?

Why do some people fall in and out of love? The pattern is a familiar one. Initially, there's a period of great love and excitement that leads quickly to disillusionment. There's truth to the observation that people who fall easily in love fall easily out of it. Repetitive patterns of moving from one relationship to another may reflect an underlying fear or anxiety concerning intimacy. After all, relationships often do not allow intimacy, which takes time and trust to develop.

There are other reasons why such destructive cycles repeat themselves. Some individuals are so desperate for love that they're willing to take all kinds of risks and settle for almost anyone who will have them or show them attention in the beginning of the relationship. Their own self-worth and happiness may yield to the powerful need to be attached, whatever the cost. Peer pressure, or an ingrained attitude learned in younger years that going out with someone is always better than being alone on a Saturday night, can seduce some people into making unwise decisions in their choice of partners.

Another common destructive cycle can occur when love is confused with sexual gratification. Both men and women sometimes use sex to relieve intolerable feelings of anxiety and loneliness. This may create a temporary illusion of love. But when it's over, there's a feeling of being used and an added snowballing loss of self-esteem.

But you don't have to be crippled by mistakes of the past. By consciously making an effort to determine what can be learned from the past, you can face and analyze what happened then so you don't repeat the same mistake over again. It's always helpful to give a close friend permission to suspend worrying about your feelings and tell you exactly what he or she perceives as truth concerning the situation. That way, you can have a real and meaningful discussion, although you must remember that what your friend tells you is subjective and may not exactly pinpoint where the problem lies. Nevertheless, for someone who really wants to explore past failures, honesty is a precious commodity.

Many people ask: "Where did I go wrong?" and "What mistakes did I make?" While these are good questions for which you need to find answers, dwelling on them can be destructive if it generates a passive self-pity. You need to use whatever knowledge you gain and move on. Use the answers you have found to fuel your determination to learn from that experience and not make the same mistakes.

Change What Hasn't Worked in the Past

Often, it isn't a matter of discovering a mistake, fixing it, and, presto, finding the perfect relationship. It's more a matter of learning what hasn't worked for you in the past and trying a different approach. It's possible that you may discover a pattern of behavior that isn't conducive to creating a relationship with another person. It isn't necessarily a mistake, although there's nothing wrong about making mistakes. We all do and, obviously, hope to learn from them. Sometimes, it's just that the mix between you and your potential partner just didn't work out. Determine if any of the following practices might be causing you some problems:

- *Bringing unrealistic expectations to a new relationship,* making them so impossible to achieve that you're setting yourself up for failure.
- *Failing to take the time to let a friendship develop first,* such as jumping into bed with someone you really don't know very well because he or she is sexy and really turns you on.
- *Allowing the sexual-passionate early stage of love to rule you.* You spend so much time making love that you really don't have a lot of time to talk or listen a great deal, so you don't know much about each other including mutual boundaries and values.

- *Falling for a partner's spontaneity and energy before deter-mining if that partner can also be a responsible and caring person.*
- *Making excuses for the other's lack of communication.* "He doesn't say much, but I know he loves me" or "She just clams up when we argue so I just give in and do what-ever she wants."
- *Interpreting jealousy and abuse to mean "We love each other."* Run away from someone who is verbally, emotion-ally, and physically abusive. It can be extremely dangerous.
- *Allowing a breakup to make you feel unworthy,* when, in fact, many breakups are entirely (or mostly) the responsi-bility of the partner.
- *Carrying the burden of a breakup that was simply out of your control,* when, actually, nobody really was at fault. It was "just one of those things."
- *Boasting and not telling the truth about yourself or are self-deprecating.* Most people don't hang around those who boast for long, and if you're not honest about yourself, how can you ever be believed? While it's all right to be modest about your accomplishments, people who are too self-deprecating are frustrating to others when a compli-ment has been honestly given but not accepted.
- *Letting your friends, parents, or adult children decide what's right for you.* You're a big kid now and nobody knows you better than you do. While it's all right to ask your family and friends for input, make up your own mind about what's right or wrong for you.

Consider honestly if you see yourself in any of the these scenarios. You don't have to tell anyone. Take this opportunity to really understand and reflect on your role in a recent breakup.

Don't Try to Make Yourself the "Perfect Person"

Although it's tempting to try to remake yourself into the "perfect person" so everyone will be clamoring for your attention, don't aim for perfection as you try to find your voice. Understand your weaknesses, but accept yourself even as you try to improve. Don't be too hard on yourself. Give yourself the acceptance you'd like others to give you. It will reveal itself in your actions, facial gestures, and voice.

Remember that nothing in nature is perfect. Each of us is unique, with many strong and wonderful aspects of our personalities, along with some not so great peculiarities. Give yourself time to learn your own imperfections. We often see them clearly in another, but rarely in ourselves. Once you become aware of your own frailties, you then are more able to correct them.

Hugh Prather notes in his now classical book, *Notes to Myself*: "I have two principal ways of discovering the areas where I fail to see myself. The first is acknowledging the qualities in others that irritate me. The second is acknowledging the comments that have made me defensive." Prather adds: "If I feel disapproval of someone, if I find myself ignoring or turning away from someone in a group, I am probably avoiding in myself what this person represents that I believe is true about me."

We find this latter quote quite telling. A number of people we interviewed for this book talked about qualities they disliked in those they had met on a first date. In many cases, we could quickly (and privately) note the same irritating traits in these individuals as well. Too bad there had been no second date. If either party had taken the time to ferret out the good points (almost everyone has a few), he or she might have gotten interested enough to try another get-together. If not, by at least being courteous to the end, each person might have passed along the date's name to someone who would be a better fit. Moral: Never burn your bridges. Your Mr. (or Ms.) Wonderful may need that bridge to find you and get to you.

We all try to act our best, especially when dating someone new. But what happens when we act out of character, creating a "presentation self" that inaccurately reflects our real selves? For example, have you ever tried to win a partner by impressing him or her with your flawless character? Are you an impatient person at heart but act as though you have the patience of Job? Do you pretend that money is no object when you're really a conservative soul at heart and your heart sank when your date ordered from the ala carte menu instead of the fixed price and you were paying? Do you act as though you love sports when you'd rather face the dentist's drill than attend one more baseball game even without extra innings?

These are shams that become increasingly difficult to maintain. They're different from "faking it until you are making it" because in faking it, you are giving yourself courage to be yourself, not someone else. On the other hand, playing a fictitious persona eventually explodes under the weight. More often, people who play at being someone else usually leave the relationship suddenly before being found out and place the blame on the other person. This destructive cycle is called setting yourself up for failure.

But this cycle can be broken. Consider the larger issue at work. Why try to misrepresent yourself in the first place? You will still have the fault or lack of interest (that you obviously wish was different since you're trying to cover it up), but now you're adding deception to the mix. It's far better to acknowledge that your impatience, for example, is a problem you recognize and that you're working on it. Ask the other person to help you become more tolerant in those situations that test your composure. Find a midway mark so you can enjoy an expensive meal once in awhile without measuring how much it costs, or agree to five innings of a baseball game or go to a hockey game where neither of you knows anything.

Add some humor, communication, and effort and you'll find that not only is your relationship working better, but you're also feeling better about yourself. The fact that you're aware of your fault or disinterest in something gives the other person an opportunity to admire your honesty and your commitment to learning new ways of overcoming this or any other unattractive trait.

Predictors of Love Disasters

Review the predictors of love disasters that follow. Think about them. Do any of them ring true to you? If you've been through any of these situations before, how can you avoid making the same mistakes in the future? Your relationship could be in for a love disaster if . . .

- It is based on myths, illusions, unreasonable expectations, and false assumptions.
- Your partner is neurotic, character disordered, self-centered, sexually perverse, on an ego trip, power hungry, or just plain disrespectful and mean.
- Love is like an addiction; possessive, madly and effusively romantic, or full of anxious despair ("I know she doesn't love me, but I'm desperately in love with her," or "I'll go crazy without him.").
- Your partner has a drug, alcohol, or gambling addiction, makes excuses, and refuses to get help.
- There are frequent and uncontrollable outbursts of anger. (Run away as fast as you can from violent relationships.)
- Your partner has difficulties handling finances, such as

paying bills late, overloading credit cards, missing alimony payments, or purchasing expensive items on a whim.

- Your partner hasn't grown up and wants you to play "mommy" or "daddy" and take care of him or her.
- Either of you is still emotionally hanging onto a past love and can't separate, especially if that former lover is deceased. When you have to compete with a ghost, you're bound to lose.
- Your partner can't express emotion or show sensitivity.

If any of these conditions apply to your relationship or potential partner, remember that the potential for the relationship to fail will be that much greater. Keep in mind, however, that even good intimate relationships can involve brief periods of panic, vanity, a constant need for reassurance, some craziness, arguments, and occasional boredom. However, whenever emotional, verbal, or physical abuse is involved, that should set off alarms of immediate concern. That person does not deserve your love.

There's No Deadline for Finding Love

Never settle for less just because you're afraid a present relationship may be your last chance. The truth is, it isn't. Don't put an arbitrary deadline on finding someone, such as "By the time I'm fifty," or "As soon as I retire." Life and love can't be measured that way and if you settle to meet a deadline, you may miss the person coming around the corner who is just what you've been looking for.

Take your time as you get to know yourself and cherish your strong points. As you grow to care more for yourself, others will care for you as well. Begin with forging friendships that may or may not develop into a deeper relationship. If a friendship does blossom into a romance, that's wonderful, if that is your desire. If it doesn't, all is not lost. You still have made a special friendship. Don't get discouraged. Remember the saying, "A journey of a thousand miles starts with a single step." Get moving!

Chapter 4

When You're
Feeling Stuck

"You may have to fight a battle more than once to win it."

—Margaret Thatcher, British prime minister from 1979–1990

DO YOU FEEL STUCK, as if you've tried to meet people and your efforts haven't been successful, or you've had a relationship that you thought was going somewhere and it didn't? You're trying to move on, but you're really stalled right now, as though you've run out of gas? Do you feel a total lack of energy from the time you drag yourself out of your bed to the moment you fall asleep? Are you experiencing an unbearable sadness, what some people call an "empty" feeling, often finding yourself pulling your car into your driveway with no recollection of driving home? Are you picking at your food because you're just not hungry anymore or gorging on everything in sight? If you've answered yes to several of these questions, you may be suffering from depression.

Almost everyone feels bad, down, or miserable occasionally. It is perfectly normal to be unhappy once in awhile. There are many times when being unhappy or profoundly sad is actually the most appropriate response, especially when someone you love dies or betrays you. It doesn't have to be the loss of a human that causes you pain, either. Don't feel embarrassed if you feel a profound sense of loss if your beloved pet dies. It's perfectly normal. We've all shed more than a few tears over the death of our cat or dog, especially one that has kept us company when we're alone.

When we use the word "depression" in this book, we mean a sense of overwhelming sadness, despair, or a sense of emptiness. These feelings can be appropriate when tragic events occur, what's called "situational depression." But when these feelings occur frequently for no apparent reason that you can think of, then it's cause for concern.

Depression often results from irrational ideas, such as blaming yourself for something that you were not responsible for—all those "should've," "could've," or "would've" situations in your life. Depression generally occurs because, for one reason or another, you feel inferior. Perhaps you relentlessly compare yourself unfavorably to others. "If I had been prettier, he would have asked me out again," or "If I drove a better car, she would have wanted to go out to dinner with me." You think of yourself as less attractive or lacking in some quality that you can't quite put your finger on. All you know is, you don't think you're as good as others, whatever "good" means. The reality is that there will always be people who are luckier, richer, better looking, or smarter than you are. Regardless of that, remember that each person is unique. No one in the world is exactly like you.

It's time to stop blaming others for making you feel inferior. As Eleanor Roosevelt once said: "No one can make you feel inferior without your consent." So you can pull back your consent. Think about it. If, instead of blaming yourself when a date doesn't call back or someone breaks up with you, you say to yourself, "Too bad. You just made a serious mistake not asking me out again," you'll feel a lot better than wasting time agonizing why the person didn't want to see you again. Forget that you just thought up a great comeback five hours after you were turned down for another date. Erase that mental tape of inferiority. It's important to deal with feelings of inferiority as early as possible because if you let them run rampant, they can lead to serious problems such as headaches, fears, obsessions, nightmares, insomnia, or a chronic state of feeling hopeless and inferior.

Rational sadness often ends up being a learning experience, however much you may have suffered. For example, you break up with your lover. You're in pain, but you make every effort not to cause others pain as well. Try to use this time to reexamine your goals in life. Keep in mind that it's very difficult to think yourself into correct acting; you need to act yourself into correct thinking. If you have difficultly doing this for yourself, ask your physician for a referral to a qualified social worker or therapist. Or sit down with your rabbi, minister, or priest—they not only received a great deal of training in counseling before they were ordained, but they also have helped many of your peers as well. Professional counselors, regardless of their training, won't think you're silly, weak, or weird. They all understand that you're human.

We All Have Bad Moods

At one time or another, we've all probably experienced bad moods, periods of depression, and falling in love with someone who doesn't love us back. True, life deals us some pretty unfair hands sometimes. But life can also be full of joys, pleasures, and excitement, and it's possible for you to alter the impact of reality by changing how you feel about it. One way is for you to acknowledge the pain of your real world by being helpful to others. By reaching out beyond your own pain, you can renew and revitalize yourself.

Self-Esteem Is Important

As you reenter the dating world, self-esteem is very important. We like the definition of self-esteem developed by the California Legislative Task Force on Self-Esteem (1990), that says, "appreciating my own worth and importance and having the character to be accountable for myself and to act responsibly toward others." But don't fall for the trap of equating self-esteem with just "feeling good about yourself." That can sometimes result in selfish, greedy, and uncaring behavior. It's surprising how many people feel good about themselves while "putting down" those around them.

Although we know that medication and/or counseling/ therapy can be helpful in treating what's known as "the blues" or a mild depression, if you feel you can handle your feelings just now without medication and would like to try to get yourself in a happier place, we advise you to try our recommendations.

Little Things Can Make a Big Difference

Here are some helpful suggestions to get you unstuck and moving back on the path to revitalization:

- *Take a walk.* Walk for five minutes and work up to thirty minutes or more. Enjoy the sights of nature as you get your body moving. You might like the feeling and let it become a habit, one that's healthy. Once you become a regular walker, you'll meet others along the way.
- *Write a friend.* Send an e-mail or snail mail to someone who's a stay-at-home or who would be surprised to hear from you. If you can't think of anyone, write to us.
- *Try something new.* Go to a flower show, a museum, an antique auction, or somewhere you rarely think of going. Look for new faces as you admire the other exhibits.

- *Take some TV time.* Watch a program on television that you wouldn't ordinarily watch, like a PBS documentary or reruns of *Seinfeld*.
- *Catch a flick.* Rent a Woody Allen film and settle down with a big bowl of popcorn. Laughter's a great cure for the blues. Or stretch your mind a bit and go see a serious movie or a foreign one with subtitles.
- *Get sporty.* Get into a new sport, either learning to play, watching it on TV, or going to the arena or stadium. So what if you don't understand the rules to soccer or hockey. You may find someone there who would love to educate you in the finer details of the game.
- *Take some quiet time.* Daydream without feeling guilty. Daydreams help you to relax and they can be fun. Just watch that they don't occupy too much of your time.
- *Make a wish list.* Write down all the things you'd like to do "someday." Declare this the "someday" and without giving the matter much thought, do one of the things on your list.
- *Explore the power of words.* Start to write that novel, play, or TV script you always thought of doing.
- *Join a play-reading group.* It's fun and you'll meet new people.
- *Switch places.* If you've been going to the same church or synagogue singles-mingles group and haven't found anyone you really enjoy being with, try another locale. Someone there may know someone who . . . well, you know the rest. Anyway, new faces always attract attention, so be one of them.
- *Challenge yourself.* Buy a magazine you wouldn't ever imagine yourself reading. Consider the *New Yorker* or *National Geographic*. Read at least two articles in it.
- *Join a book club.* You'll not only enjoy the opportunity to read some wonderful books, but you'll find talking about them

and exchanging ideas at this time in your life is a lot more fun than it may have seemed in school.

• *Get a furry friend.* Go to the Humane Society and adopt a dog or cat. If you want a pet with less upkeep, visit the tropical fish store and stock your personal aquarium.

• *Find a hobby.* For example, take up gardening and grow some plants—flowers, herbs, or vegetables—even if you've never thought you had a green thumb. No excuse that you live in a high rise, either. There are all kinds of flowers and herbs you can grow in pots. You then can meet all kinds of new friends and join conversations to learn about mulch, fertilizer, and rock gardens. Or decide to collect something, depending on your available space at home. The choices are wide open, from egg cups to antique medical instruments, to dreidels, coins, or stamps.

• *Join a gym.* It's hard to be depressed when you're balancing on a ball or lifting weights. Sign up for yoga or tai chi classes. Both are good for balance as well as meeting new people.

• *Meditate.* If you don't know how, read Herbert Benson's *Relaxation Response* (see the Suggested Reading section at the back of the book for publishing information).

• *Keep learning.* Read an article in the newspaper that will give you some new information. Buy a foreign newspaper and see how much of your high school Spanish or French you remember.

• *Communicate.* Renew a friendship that you've neglected. Risk its working or not working out.

• *Get artistic.* Make a collage from old family photos. Paint a garage-sale wooden chair in fun colors. Make a mobile for your room. Put on an old shirt, cover a table with newspapers, and start finger-painting.

• *Try culinary therapy.* Make a casserole for a shut-in or bake something—bread, cookies, or a cake—for someone else.

If you're in an organization, volunteer to cook or serve at a meeting. Cooking brings good friends together with laughter mixed in.

• *Get a massage or pedicure.* This type of "good" touching not only feels good, but also has therapeutic benefit because it aids circulation.

• *Volunteer.* One of the best things you can do when you're sad and lonely is to volunteer your services for the benefit of others without expecting anything in return. We call it "mitzvah therapy" and we both are into it.

Why Mitzvah Therapy Works

"Mitzvah" comes from the Hebrew word "miṣwāh" and refers to a meritorious or charitable act. Mitzvah therapy is a helpful alternative or addition to counseling. For example, Clara, a very bright woman, had been in therapy for five years. She had been abused as a child, said she had no friends, and was depressed and sometimes considered suicide as a way out of her unhappiness. She begged her therapist for help and he suggested that Clara become a volunteer at a home for abused children.

At first, Clara was hesitant, feeling she had no qualities the children would relate to. But after one month of volunteering on an almost daily basis, she reported that she had never felt happier in her whole life. What's more, for the first time she felt needed, wanted, and appreciated. Even more exciting to her, the children at the home adored her, and she realized that she didn't have to start out loving herself just to be helpful and loving to others in need.

Something else occurred. After Clara's first week at the children's home, she met another volunteer there—a man. He was short (meaning shorter than she was), bald, and, she admitted, "kind of ugly." But they became friends and she looked forward to coming to the children's home to see him as well as the children. He was still short and bald, but after a couple of months of friendship, she said, "I can't imagine why I thought he was ugly. He's nice looking and we like and enjoy each other."

Mitzvahs are a wonderful way to overcome that "stuck" feeling. When you feel respected, needed, wanted, and appreciated by others, you'll be amazed how you'll begin to feel love for yourself and have the capacity to love others.

Do You Still Feel Stuck?

If you've tried the works—Internet dating, singles events, walking the dog, astrological signs, late-night supermarket shopping, dates set up by friends and relatives—and nothing seems to get you out of your funk, here are a bunch of maybes that might be holding you back:

- You're looking for the wrong person (a myth model).
- You haven't learned what you really want out of life. Take time to think about it and write it down so you can refresh your memory from time to time.
- Your expectations are unreasonable. You're looking for the perfect person and are too critical of minor imperfections everyone (including you) has.
- You keep thinking something must be wrong with the person you're dating. Why isn't he or she married at this point?
- You feel deep down that it's hopeless; you'll always be alone.
- You look and act exhausted and grim. You don't smile very often.

- You can't resist telling your troubles to your date, even on the first meeting.
- Worse than anything else, you feel that you don't deserve what you want. You're still playing negative tapes created by others, perhaps as far back as your parents and/or teachers, and accepting them as the gospel truth.

Don't despair. It "ain't over yet." True, it's not easy to move in a new direction and old habits are difficult to break, but they can be broken. As you read this book and move on to new steps in your life, make an effort to stop all the things that haven't worked for you in the past. They're behind you and cannot be changed, so empty your mind of them and think about your present life. What energizes you?

There are plenty of ways to boost your energy and your optimism. Consider any of the following:

- *Exercise every day.* If you can't go to a gym for a workout, walk for at least half an hour at least five days a week. If you can afford a personal trainer, sign up with one for four to six sessions to get you started. If you can't, get a friend to join you so you'll have no excuse to forgo your workout.
- *Lose weight if you need to.* Try Weight Watchers or the Atkins Diet or the South Beach Diet, but first get approval from your physician, especially if you have specific ailments or chronic disorders.
- *Develop a passionate interest or hobby.* Find something you can share with others. This does not include television, romance novels, or gossip.
- *Create reasonable goals for yourself.* You can't try to be the best cook in town, have the cleanest home, volunteer on twenty boards, and still find time for relaxation and

rejuvenation. You may be so busy trying to be all things to everyone that you have no time to be yourself or to seek out new friendships. Perhaps the reason you're having difficulty finding someone new in your life is that you're keeping yourself too busy so you have an excuse if you don't find anyone. Weed out some of those commitments and make time in your life for possibilities.

- *Stop the worry cycle.* Our advice: Plan ahead, don't worry ahead. Try this:
  - If a worry enters your mind, mentally say "stop" and focus on something else. You can't hold two thoughts in your mind at the same time.
  - If you still find yourself worrying constantly, set aside five minutes each day to worry.
  - If a concern pops into your head before your assigned "worry time," jot it down to focus on during your set worry period. You'll soon find that it does little good to worry and that you can find better use of those five minutes.
- *Stop trying to please everyone.* You must first please yourself and thereafter only those people you care about. People who try to please everyone end up pleasing no one (and being very frustrated and depressed).

Learning to Feel Good about Yourself

Are you looking for the meaning of life? Life is not a meaning; it is an opportunity. Life is made up of meaningful experiences that are mainly of short duration, but are (happily) repeatable. You can usually control your attitude about the difficult circumstances of your life. More often than not, it is your attitude that makes the difference. Everyone has burdens in life, but it's the way you carry them that makes the difference. People who feel good about themselves . . .

- Are enthusiastic about life.
- Have a good sense of humor, but never use it to be hurtful.
- Like to try new experiences.
- Have a variety of interests.
- Are good listeners.
- Accept what they can't change and make the best of it.
- Look for opportunities to help others through volunteerism.
- Are unselfish.
- Don't exploit others.
- Don't allow themselves to be exploited.
- Don't make fun of others.
- Seek the purpose of their life and then try to live it.
- Are resilient.
- Don't gossip.
- Are hopeful.
- Are willing to take risks.
- Encourage others to feel good about themselves as well.

How can you feel good about yourself? You can start by creating a miracle for yourself. Recognize that you are unique, and stop comparing yourself with other people. Believe that you can stand on your own merits. Philosopher and theologian Martin Buber, reflecting on the philosophy of the Baal Shem Tov, the great Hasidic master, suggested that every person born into this world represents something new, something that never existed before. Think about your own special gift, because it's there; you just may never have recognized it. All of us have the task of actualizing our unprecedented and never-recurring potentiality and not the repetition of something that another has already achieved. Everyone is unique. You have to feel that you are someone special in order to become attractive to others. You have to accept yourself before you can please someone you care about. You have to accept your uniqueness in this world.

In his book *Man's Search for Meaning*, psychiatrist and Holocaust survivor Viktor E. Frankl suggests that we shouldn't aim for success. The more you aim at it and make it a target, the more you are going to miss it. It's true that success is like happiness—it cannot be pursued. It lights on your shoulders as you go about your business of helping others. It becomes the unintended side effect of one's personal dedication to a cause greater than oneself. Golf instructors tell their clients, "Don't look at the ball; look at where you want it to go." The same is true for how each of us should go about our business, looking toward where we want to go, and trusting that happiness and success will follow.

When Does Being Depressed Become Serious Depression?

Sometimes, with the best of intentions, you just can't get out of your depression. It's not just "the blues," and you really feel stuck. When should you seek medical attention? Most experts agree that depression should be of concern when it interferes with a person's daily functioning and when it continues over too long a period of time. But how much "interference" is too much and how long is "a long period of time"? Unfortunately, there is no blood test to take in order to get a diagnosis of depression. It's a continuum disorder, ranging from the blues at one end and a feeling of despair and weariness at the other end, with a great deal of variation in between these two extremes.

If you're depressed, you may not even be aware of it. It may come on gradually as you allow the laundry and newspapers to pile up, forget about eating, and don't bother to change into clean clothes. You may look sad and withdraw from activities you used to enjoy. According to William S. Pollack, assistant clinical professor at Harvard Medical School, in an article in the July 2003 *Prevention* magazine, men sometimes display different signs of depression from women. He says depressed men "[become] workaholics or lose their tempers, flying into rage with little provocation . . . gamble irresponsibly, take risks, [turn] to drugs or alcohol." If you're displaying any of the symptoms mentioned and you don't recognize them yourself, hopefully you have adult children or friends who will urge you to seek medical help. Please take their advice.

What Are the Specific Signs of Depression?

The American Psychiatric Association has set up some very specific criteria to be used to make the diagnosis of major depression. The following signs have been adapted from their guidelines:

1. Persistent mood of discomfort: depression, feeling low or irritable, showing signs of hopelessness, including a loss of interest in things and a loss of a sense of pleasure.
2. At least four of the following symptoms for at least two weeks:
   - Poor appetite or weight loss (or increased appetite or weight gain).
   - Change in sleeping habits, such as insomnia, waking up earlier, or sleeping for long periods of time.

- Psychomotor agitation (such as pacing, sighing, or wringing hands) or motor retardation (slowdown of motions).
- Loss of interest in normal activities or decrease in sexual drive.
- Loss of energy.
- Feelings of worthlessness, inadequacy, or excessive (and inappropriate) guilt.
- Reduced concentration or indecisiveness.
- Thought of death or actual suicide attempts.

Obviously, use of the these criteria, which have been adapted from *Diagnostic and Statistical Manual of Mental Disorders* (2000), is based on your observations. Your conclusion, therefore, is subjective. But trust your instinct and don't censor your gut instinct. Listen to your body, and if you suspect that you (or a loved one) is depressed, based on what you sense (or see in another), and it lasts for two weeks or more, there's a good chance that it is depression.

While you may be in denial and make excuses, such as "Of course I'm tired all the time. I'm getting old," or "It's just too hot to eat. I don't have much of an appetite anymore," be aware that you may be masking your symptoms because you're embarrassed to admit that you could be depressed. There is nothing to be ashamed of. Depression isn't a sign of weakness. What's more, your symptoms, which may seem like depression, could actually be reactions to some of the medications you're taking for high blood pressure, arthritis, or other chronic conditions. As we get older, our kidney and liver metabolize these medications more slowly, so they stay in our system longer. These drugs also may be interacting adversely with other medications—prescription, over-the-counter, and herbal remedies. The point is, if you're showing signs of depression for whatever reason, do seek medical care from a qualified health care professional.

Good News about Depression

Yes, there is good news about depression, and that is, depression usually is transitory. That means the old saying "Even this shall pass" is true. There are steps, however, that you can take to give wings to the blues. Try a few of our suggestions and see how they work for you.

Remember the Importance of the Power of Touch

If you're between romances, you may be missing a soothing touch. But touches need not be sexual. You can ask for and receive comforting informal touches through shampoos, manicures, and massages, by going to dances and enjoying the physical contact your partner provides, or even by joining a sports team where hugging and patting by team members is accepted.

Our language is filled with expressions that attest to the importance of touch, such as "Lend a helping hand," "Reach out," "Just the right touch," and "That's touching." Sherry Suib Cohen, coauthor of *The Magic of Touch,* has this to say about touching: "You can't give a touch without getting one right back. You can talk, listen, smell, see, and taste alone, but touch is a reciprocal act."

Remember to Smile

Try an experiment. Walk into any mall and smile at the shoppers. You'll find many of them smiling back at you. We all respond to smiles. Think how delighted adults are when they think a baby has smiled at them! You'll also find people respond more to you when you're smiling, even when you feel you have nothing to smile about. The late Lucille Ball said: "One of the things I learned the hard way was that it doesn't pay to get discouraged. Keeping busy and making optimism a way of life can restore your faith in yourself." It also attracts other people to you.

Surround yourself with people who are optimistic and find fun and humor in life. Spend as little time as possible with non-smilers and make sure you're not one of them.

Remember to Practice Relaxation Techniques

Each person must determine which of the many relaxation techniques works best for him or her, but the important point is to find one or more and do them. There is progressive relaxation, yoga, meditation, and visualization, just to mention a few. There are numerous books and tapes available to help you, some of which are listed in the back of this book. Western physicians, after years of being skeptical, are finally accepting that these modalities can help many physical conditions, including depression.

Remember to Plan for Daily Exercise

It's hard to feel down after a fast walk, swim, or game of doubles. You not only feel better when you've exercised, but you look better, too. Exercise, whatever its form, chases away fatigue and its ever-present companion, depression.

Take time to determine what type of exercise you like because if you don't enjoy it, you won't continue to do it. That said, be open to trying new types of exercise, such as canoeing, aerobics, biking, softball, or weight lifting. Don't buy expensive equipment like skis and ski outfits, ten-speed bikes, or weight machines until you know that's the type of exercise you like.

Investigate health clubs so you know you'll like the equipment and the people who frequent the one you decide to join. While home treadmills and stair-climbing machines may be more convenient to use, you'll miss the interaction with other people that's also important to your well-being.

Remember That You Can Initiate a Friendship

Even if you're a little shy by nature, there's nothing wrong with being friendly and asking someone to join you for a cup of coffee, go on a bike ride, or give advice on your golf swing. If you hold back, waiting for others to make the first move, you may miss the opportunity to cultivate a new friendship, and possibly lose a potential partner.

Chapter 5

How Media Fashions
Our Perceptions

"Everywhere we turn, we're faced with glamorized,
idealized versions of love. It's as if the culture wants us to
stay trapped in the fantasy and does everything possible
to encourage and expand that fantasy."

—Florence Falk, New York City psychotherapist

DR. FALK'S ABSOLUTELY RIGHT. Look at the magazines on the
newsstand. In one there's an article about how a man's nose,
eyes, and mouth can reveal (in six seconds) his love potential. In
others, "11 Sex Moves Men Wish We'd Try," "Feel Close to Him
All Over Again (A Lover's Guide)," "50 Sexy Surprises," "Sizzling
Sex," and even "Sexy Spring Shoes."

Still another magazine predicts: "Soon there may be a medicine for couples to enhance love." The height of silliness
emerges in newspapers around Valentine's Day. For example, an
article in a February 1999 issue of the *San Francisco Chronicle*
writes about "our pheromone cloud," suggesting that a whiff of
another person's pheromones, a substance secreted externally
that affects behavior (usually described in insects!), can predict
whether or not we'll fall in love or be repelled by that person.

While no one doubts the effects of human pheromones on
sexual behavior, to suggest that "if he smells good, go for him,"
is, at best, simplistic. You'd think we've all lived long enough to

be immune to this type of doggerel. But still we buy the magazines, watch the television talk shows, and feel the message
must be true because the media says so and, after a pause, we
muse, what's the matter with us?

We've all been brain-washed by the media from the time we
all were little and heard fairy tales of romantic love—from
Cinderella who gets out of the kitchen and gets the prince
(Always a handsome one. Who gets the slightly portly princes,
we wonder?) to the movie *Pretty Woman,* where another
Cinderella gets out of the bed and gets her successful business
executive (also handsome).

There's no doubt that mass media are powerful socialization
agents, both subconsciously and consciously. Sex and body
image messages assault us, not only from television and the
movies, but also from books and magazines, music, radio, advertising, and even the news. One study reveals that afternoon soap
operas contained thirty-five instances of sexual content per hour,
or more than one instance every two minutes. In all program cat-
egories, unmarried heterosexual couples engage in sexual intercourse from four to eight times more frequently than married
men and women, and partners seldom if ever contract sexually
transmitted diseases, let alone discuss "safe sex." It's only natural
to consider these statistics and wonder why you aren't getting
your fair share of sexual contacts.

There's no doubt that pressure mounts as we age, as we're
continually bombarded by messages of youth, slimness, and sexuality while we look in the mirror and see thinning hair,
drooping breasts and buttocks, wrinkles, and a thickening waist,
amidst new aches and pains. The reality is clear: Our opportunity to become the *Playboy* or *Playgirl* centerfold has passed us
by. No wonder the expectations assaulting us from the media
can create depression, loss of confidence, and even sexual
dysfunction.

We all have the "Perfect Body" image in our heads. Magazines, movies, and television bombard us with the messages that being thin for women and muscular for men will almost always guarantee success and fulfillment. Anything about us that deviates from that image is viewed by ourselves in an exaggerated way—whether it is our nose, thighs, arms, or total body weight. Diet and fitness programs that "guarantee" sure and quick results reinforce the current ideal image, but most don't work. Yet, how many new diets have you tried in the last few years?

Obviously, if you're overweight, it is within your ability to change your diet by cutting down on foods high in sugar and those offering low nutritional value. It's essential to eat fish, vegetables, fruit, and nuts to maintain good health. This, combined with regular exercise, can bring your weight down. You may find it helpful to join an exercise class or a recognized weight-loss program such as Weight Watchers or Overeaters Anonymous. There you'll learn the triggers that make you revert to overeating, such as stress and emotions. You'll also discover alternative ways to reduce tension, such as an active hobby, a sport activity such as biking, walking, swimming, or jogging, or yoga or meditation. Remember, however, that the models you see on television and in the ads often starve themselves to remain thin (the camera does add weight, unfortunately) and they often have personal trainers to help them get the most from their exercise time.

But getting thin or fit doesn't automatically help you make friends. While you often can't change certain aspects of your appearance, you can change your attitude about *how* you look. People who accept themselves are attractive to other people. It's not true that only attractive people find mates, but it is true that people who hate themselves or dissect disliked areas ("I hate my thighs," "I hate my sagging stomach," or "I hate my drooping breasts") tend to repel rather than attract others.

It's easy to blame what in your mind is your less than perfect appearance or some imagined physical "defects" you have for the present lack of romance in your life, but it's time to face reality. Instead of finding physical defects and moaning that the actors and actresses you see on television have it all, focus instead on your personality, your generosity, your curiosity for learning, your caring for others, and all the other good qualities you possess that are not related to your looks. Frankly, we know a great many overweight, short, and balding people who have good relationships and happy marriages. Don't you? And they're not on the silver screen. They live in real time. It's time to begin to embrace the wonderful variety of variations of the human body.

Reality Pales in Hollywood

For many individuals, a striking gap exists between the public image of love and their personal history of it. Since Hollywood images usually depict love as sensational and glamorous, they do not even remotely resemble most of our private experience. Thus, feelings of inadequacy and internal conflicts can easily develop, and you may find yourself asking, "Why does my relationship seem so boring when compared to what everyone else seems to have?"

Romance is a wonderful thing, but life isn't like the romantic images that appear in movies, on TV, or in advertisements. It's something many people simply have to get over when they become adults. For example, here's screenwriter Delia Ephron recalling her reaction to the film *Seven Brides for Seven Brothers*. "All I wanted to do was be this woman making flapjacks for these guys who don't even take a bath. Your ideas of being swept away and romance and some of the worst aspects of love are formed when you're a child. And this desire to swoon is really fed by these movies you see when young, and when you're older that feeling is validated over and over again."

You may think you don't agree with Ms. Ephron, but if you're a woman, remember the first time you saw Clark Gable swoop Vivian Leigh up in his arms and take her upstairs or Burt Lancaster on the beach with Deborah Kerr in *From Here to Eternity.* Wasn't there a tingle then and a yearning, yes, even now, to find someone who would want you that much? If you're a man, what about Lauren Bacall whispering in her husky, sensuous voice: "Just pucker up your lips and blow. You know how to do that, don't you?"

Yes, the movies and television conjure up in our minds the way people act or *should* act when they're in love and we tend to be just a little disappointed when our partner doesn't act like Denzel Washington, Mel Gibson, Robert Redford, or Halle Berry, Catherine Zeta-Jones, or Sela Ward. Therefore, you need to examine your ideas about romance and love. Are they creating problems for you by being unrealistic? Are they creating unfair and unjust expectations from imperfect, but loving human beings who may indeed be right for you, given the chance? Romance is like water; we all need it in our lives. But it makes sense to strive for a balance in your life, to allow reality to enhance your notion of romance. That way, a deeply loving relationship will have a chance to develop into a lasting one.

If life is often not like media images portraying it, neither are the actors' lives. A number of years ago, a young woman and her husband met the acting greats Hume Cronin and Jessica Tandy for a business meeting. "We had tea at their home in Canada," Carol recalled. "The men talked business while I chatted with Jessica Tandy. I had seen many of her plays and found her to be delightful in person. When I had to use the toilet, she directed me upstairs to their bathroom. I shut the door: There was reality. Jessica Tandy's nightgown hung on the back of the door. It startled me at first to realize that, as famous as she was, her nightgown was on the back of the door, hanging just like mine and those of millions of other women." That's what we have to remember. The movie and theater stars are just human beings, albeit with publicists whose job it is to get their names in the media.

More than one movie star—Tom Cruise, Nicole Kidman, Tom Hanks, Susan Sarandon—is quoted in magazines and on late-night television as picking up their kids from school, doing homework with them, and helping with the cooking and other chores. While it may be hype and good copy from their publicist, it's probably true that their real lives turn out to be made of much of the same stuff all of us experience. On one hand, the illusion you've held of the particular movie star's life is shattered. You don't really want that star to admit to doing the mundane everyday activities we all do. It makes him or her seem so, well, so *ordinary*. But, on the other hand, reading about these stars' lives full of joy and satisfaction that comes from enriching relationships (even though they often don't last long in Hollywood) with a partner and children also provides us with a tonic of hope. It means that their so-called "glamorous" lives are potentially attainable by all of us.

To once again quote Florence Falk: "Trying to forge an authentic relationship amidst all the romantic hype makes what is already a tough proposition even harder."

Media Sex Is Irresponsible
A report commissioned by the Kaiser Family Foundation titled "Measuring the Effects of Sexual Content in the Media" investigated sexual messages in movies and on television in prime time, soaps, and music videos. (You can view this report

at *www.kff.org.*) Although the original intent of the study was to investigate the effects of sexual content in the media on children and adolescents, a great deal of the information has importance to adults as well. For example, according to the study, "There has been an overall increase in the number of portrayals and the amount of talk about sex in these media and an increase in the explicitness of these portrayals. Furthermore, the television research shows a fairly consistent sexual message across TV genres: Most portrayals of sex depict or imply heterosexual intercourse between unmarried adults, with little reference to STDs/AIDS, pregnancy, or use of contraception."

Think about some of the television shows you enjoy. *Friends* and *Sex and the City* show young adults hopping in and out of beds without any mention of safe sex. One of the characters on *Frasier* is equally irresponsible as the running gag throughout the show concerns the number of sexual partners she's had. In the long running series *Seinfeld,* all of the characters (except, perhaps, George) had numerous affairs, one-night stands included, with never a mention of any attempt to practice safe sex.

What does that mean to us? It creates expectations that it's okay to have spur-of-the-moment sex without being careful to know the sexual history of the partner or taking precautions to prevent sexually transmitted diseases. It also creates the expectation that "everyone's doing it" without really getting to know his or her partner very well.

Can You Pass the Mass Media Test?
Dr. Mary-Lou Galician (rhymes with "physician") is an award-winning mass media researcher, educator, and performer who teaches courses in mass media and "Love and Romance in the Mass Media" at Arizona State University's Walter Cronkite

School. Her newest book, *Dr. Galician's Prescriptions for Getting Real about Romance: How Mass Media Myths about Love Can Hurt You*, examines how mass media portrayals of sex, love, and romance affect nearly all of us, even though we may not be aware of it. "People in my studies with unrealistic expectations are less satisfied in their own romantic relationships," says Galician, "and many of these unrealistic expectations come from media we enjoy without duly considering how they influence us at a subconscious level."

To further her point, Dr. Fun, as she is known, has compiled what she calls "Dr. Fun's Mass Media Love Quiz." It appears on page ix of *Sex, Love, and Romance in the Mass Media: Analysis and Criticism of Unrealistic Portrayals and Their Influence*. We use it with her permission. How well do you do?

Please mark "True" or "False" for each statement:

	True	False
1. Your perfect partner is cosmically predestined for you and nothing/nobody can ultimately separate you.	❐	❐
2. There's such a thing as "love at first sight."	❐	❐
3. Your true "soul mate" knows what you're thinking or feeling without your having to tell.	❐	❐
4. If your partner is truly meant for you, sex is easy and wonderful.	❐	❐
5. To attract and keep a man, a woman should look like a model or centerfold.	❐	❐
6. The man should *not* be shorter, weaker, younger, poorer, or less successful than the woman.	❐	❐
7. The love of a good and faithful true	❐	❐

woman can change a man from a
"beast" into a "prince."

8. Bickering and fighting a lot mean that ☐ ☐
   a man and a woman really love each
   other passionately.

9. All you really need is love, so it doesn't ☐ ☐
   matter if you and your partner have
   very different values.

10. The right mate "completes you"—filling ☐ ☐
    your needs and making your dreams
    come true.

11. In real life, actors are very much like ☐ ☐
    the romantic characters they portray.

12. Since mass media portrayals of romance ☐ ☐
    aren't "real," they don't really affect you.

If you answered "false" to all the above statements, you pass
and receive an "R" (for realistic). "The problem is," says Dr.
Galician, "that while most of us 'know' the 'right' responses to
these quiz items, we still 'believe' the unrealistic ones our popular culture presents to us."

Monkey See, Monkey Don't Do

Think about the sex and violence you have seen in movies and
on television. We see it so often that we have the tendency to
almost overlook it as commonplace, yet the images do affect us
emotionally and can affect our attitude and even our behavior
toward sexual violence.

Never consider or make excuses that physical, verbal, or
emotional violence is a sign of love. Jackie Gleason on television's *The Honeymooners* was never funny to some of us as he

told his wife Alice, "One of these days, Alice . . . ," and then he'd make a hitting gesture. Violence is just that, violence, plain and simple. If you meet someone who has a history of domestic violence, walk away. He or she is unlikely to change behavior in a new relationship with you. No, not even if you're sweet, lovable, and kind, you won't change this individual. He or she will continue in the old ways and say you made him (or her) do it (be violent). You'll find yourself feeling guilty for being a victim!

Media's Messages

So how do we handle all this nonreality we see, read, and hear? Start with an open mind and be thankful you're no longer a teenager who has to deal with it along with raging hormones. It's unlikely that things will change, so we'll all continue to see sizzling sex sold in the media. To be truthful, sometimes if you're in a relationship, it can be quite a turn-on. So what if he's imagining he's with Halle Berry and she's visualizing Sean Connery?

Just remember not to compare yourself to the pictures you see, the statistics you hear, or the studies you read. After all, those kinds of figures *do* lie. Everyone lies about their sexual prowess, even (and especially) to sex researchers. Have fun when you read a steamy scene in a chapter of a best-seller, but don't hold it up as an example of what everyone else is doing and feel you need to pattern your behavior after it. You don't. Be true to what seems comfortable and moral for you.

If explicit sex scenes in movies and on television make you uncomfortable, walk out or switch channels, although who knows, you may pick up a sensual trick or two. If explicit sex scenes in movies bother you, don't go. Change channels on your television if you don't like what's being shown. The same goes for violence and other disturbing scenes in movies and on television. Put yourself in charge of what you read, see, or hear in the media. The media serves you, not the other way around. There's nothing wrong in enjoying watching the energy and good health of young bodies in ads without envy and, yes, even buying those sexy shoes if you want them.

Just remember that you're the police not the prisoner when dealing with the media. You enforce what's important to you, not what you're spoon-fed. You're the important message here.

Chapter 6

Finding Friends and Knowing When It's Special

"Friendship is born at the moment when one person says to another, What! You, too? I thought I was the only one.'"

—C. S. Lewis (1898–1963), English novelist and essayist

YOU, TOO, CAN FIND that moment. To do so, however, you must remember that friendship is different from love, although you need true friendship in a love relationship as well. But first, friendship is what you're looking for.

True Friendships Take Time to Grow

There's no doubt that it's difficult to think about dating again after being in a long-term relationship. It's bound to feel a little weird at first. You may feel like Rip Van Winkle when you look around and see how things have changed in the dating game. For one, the rules have changed. For example, men no longer automatically pay for the date. The man may pay for dinner and the woman the theater, or vice versa. The woman today often pays for the entire date, especially if she has done the inviting. In addition, the onus is no longer on the man to call a woman for a date. Forget that your mother said, "Nice girls don't call boys."

Today they do, and in many cases the men are actually relieved that someone other than themselves made the move.

When you meet someone whose company you enjoy—and the feeling is reciprocated—it's tempting to rush ahead to the next level of intimacy. But don't. Go slowly and savor the pleasure this growing friendship offers. Remember that the tortoise took his time, too, but eventually he won the race. Fortunately, you're not in a race, whatever your age. You can afford to relax and enjoy the moment. Spend time getting to know each other's likes and dislikes, values, history, and interests. Remain aware of your comfort level so you can decide if you want to remain "just friends" or to move into a relationship where you become more intimate. Focus first on friendship and see where that ship takes you.

In her 1987 book, *Straight from the Heart*, Carol Cassell wrote: "Love is friendship, sparked by sexual chemistry, that grows over time." It also takes time for these special friendships that may develop into love to be nourished and to grow, like a beautiful flower, a treasured painting, or any other work of art. So don't be in a rush. It seems we're all so used to rushing things, moving faster and faster, that we miss much of life's joys. We read condensed books, eat fast foods, and relish being the One-Minute whatever, and forget to slow down to enjoy life as well as new friendships as they unfold. When we hurry, we tend to make mistakes.

Make Someone—Yourself—Happy

In the twenty-fifth anniversary edition of his book *The Road Less Traveled*, M. Scott Peck, M.D., warns that "If being loved is your goal, you will fail to achieve it. The only way to be assured of being loved is to be a person worthy of love, and you cannot be a person worthy of love when your primary goal in life is to passively be loved." By that, Dr. Peck means that we need to be less dependent on others to make us happy and learn how to be happy in our own skin. Only then can we reach out to others.

You may think it's difficult to be happy with all the difficult troubles you've gone through, such as a divorce, death of a spouse, or the breakup of a relationship for which you really had high hopes. But that was in the past and, as you know, the past can't be changed, although we all often wish it could be. The father of our country, George Washington, wrote: "We ought not to look back unless it is to derive useful lessons from past errors, and for the purpose of profiting by dear bought experience." And, as you might remember, "Father knows best."

You are the only person who can make yourself happy today, and that's by making up your mind that you'll focus on something good, optimistic, and upbeat. That's why we suggest helping others, doing activities that fulfill you, and discovering the things that make you smile. Make that symbolic glass half full, not half empty, and you'll be more likely to find others attracted to you by your positive outlook on life.

You have plenty of time, even if you're in your fifties, sixties, seventies, or even eighties. Don't think you've passed what one woman referred to as "the dating age." There is no age limitation in the way the game's played today. It used to be that an individual—usually a woman, widowed or divorced—in her fifties or sixties figured that "that part" of her life was over and that she'd never find another companion, so she settled down to babysit grandchildren, live through her children, and watch the daytime soaps on television. Not so now. Today, that person is probably out playing tennis doubles, golfing, skiing in Colorado, jogging, lifting weights in the gym, attending seminars, or having Botox injections to make those few wrinkles disappear, and checking out the landscape for someone new.

According to a report by the American Association of Retired Persons (AARP), today at age fifty, Americans can generally expect to be healthy for another thirty years. People age eighty-five and older are the fastest growing segment of U.S. seniors. So never think you're too old to find a companion.

But the standards that many people require when looking for love—beauty, big bucks, and power—carry little weight in a best-buddy relationship. There are more subtle criteria for a best-buddy friendship, such as caring, trust, humor, and reliability, especially in a friendship that has the potential to develop into a lasting relationship. When you go looking for friendship with these values, you may find that you've not only found a special friend, but someone whom you can and will love. Sounds good, you say, but where do you find these people?

Potential Friends Are Doing Something

Chances are, the people you'd like to meet aren't sitting home watching television or feeling sorry for themselves. They're active individuals. Look for meeting new friends where you volunteer, work, or do mitzvahs (good deeds), whether it's in schools, hospitals, rehab centers, or even overseas (like the Peace Corps and Doctors Without Borders).

Doing Ordinary Chores

You can meet people doing ordinary daily chores at Laundromats, hardware stores, and grocery stores. In stores such as Home Depot, women often ask pertinent questions of men who look interesting and act as though they know the difference between a Phillips screwdriver and an awl, while men return the

favor at the grocery, asking how to fix acorn squash or arti-
chokes, explaining that "Now that I'm alone, it's hard to know
how to fix these things." You, too, can meet people doing the
same everyday chores that keep you busy and at many of the
same places. Your neighborhood supermarket is an excellent
place to make friends because you tend to see many of the same
faces shopping at the same time you are. A nod one week may
become a smile the next, and before you know it, the man you
always see in the organic vegetable department might say hello,
confess that he's a gourmet cook, and admit he'd like a companion for dinner.

Always remember to go slowly in this type of a relationship,
though, and meet at first only in public places. Don't give out
your address at first, and never assume that just because
someone looks nice and dresses well, it is safe to be alone with
him or her. Unfortunately, there are people who prey on single
individuals.

Harry, then seventy-two, and Florence, then sixty-one, sat
next to each other on an airplane from Atlanta to Tampa. "She
took a book out," Harry recalled. "I said, 'Oh, I see you like
Sidney Sheldon.' She put the book away and we talked the rest
of the trip. We exchanged phone numbers. Over the next four
years, we often met for lunch at a shopping center. I never went
to her home as she was suspicious and felt more comfortable
meeting in public. We both were involved with other people at
the time. Then, both of our former relationships went 'on the
fritz' at the same time. I liked her as a friend so asked her out for
dinner. She accepted, and this time let me pick her up at her
house. Her sister was there to be sure I didn't try anything
'funny.' We continued to date, meeting at the shopping center. I
had to get my passport renewed. The marriage license place was
at the same counter. Next time I saw Florence, I said, 'No way
we're going to get married. The license costs $64.' The next day,

I received a card from her with a check for $32. Four years after we had met, we got married. I was seventy-six and Florence was sixty-five. We've now been married ten years. I think we had to be friends first."

Working at a Part-Time Job

Freelance writer, L. N., suggests that you "get a part-time retail job in a good specialty shop. Flirt! I'm on my third romantic adventure that began this way. One was a dud. Two, we'll see. Also, go to industry events. At a press party I met a fellow journalist. We'll see. I'm dating *way* past regular dating age. [Authors' note: There *is* no regular dating age.] I'm looking for friendship, fun, good conversation, and intimacy, the latter only if the chemistry conditions are right."

Browsing in Bookstores

Bookstores also are good places to make friends. You'll know the folks you meet are literate, and if you find them in the same section you're browsing, you probably have some interests in common. Many bookstores welcome patrons by setting up tables and easy chairs and selling coffee, sandwiches, and cookies just to keep patrons in the stores longer.

Going to Video Stores

While you can meet people at video stores, they usually don't stroll as leisurely as they do in bookstores. Most people find a tape or DVD, grab it off the shelf before anyone else gets the last copy, and get in line to pay for it. You can, however, start up a conversation by asking someone's opinion about a particular movie. But if you're into British dramas and the other person has a Power Ranger or motorcycle film, you might think twice.

You may see familiar faces at your neighborhood video store, especially on Friday night when everyone stocks up for the weekend. If you see someone you'd like to get to know better looking at a video or DVD that you've seen, there's nothing wrong with saying something like "that was a great movie." If that person is interested, he or she might ask you more about it. At least you know that you both have movies in common. But if the other person checks out a stack of movies with violence and car crashes and you're into British dramas, just smile and say "Enjoy the movie" and move along.

Walking the Dog

Meeting someone while walking your dog may sound silly at first, but not to dog lovers. Walking your dog is a terrific way to open conversations because dogs, like kittens and babies, cause strangers (who also like dogs) to smile, stop, and ask doggie questions of other perfect strangers. Dogs are terrific icebreakers, even in communities where no one makes eye contact. If your area is fortunate enough to have a dog park where dogs can run free, you'll soon become a regular and can meet other dog lovers and chat without being self-conscious. You'll have another plus as well. Walking your dog is a great way to exercise and even lose a little weight.

Going to Bars

What about going to a bar? Usually we don't think that's the place to meet someone new. It's too hard to see in the dark, there's usually too much noise to make interesting conversation, it's filled with people who have had too much to drink, and do you really want to twirl on a bar stool all night? On the other hand, if there's a nice quiet pub with soft music where you could have a glass of wine and talk, then you might go with some friends to see who else is there.

Shopping

Obviously, you can't spend all day hanging out at a store, waiting for someone interesting to walk by. But one woman we interviewed said she found her "significant other" at an optical shop. "He was trying on glasses and asked what I thought. I said it made him look intellectual, like a college professor. It turns out he was both an intellectual and a college professor. We kept talking, had coffee, started dating, and as they say, the rest is history."

Giving a Singles Party

Why advertise that you're single and looking? Because parties are the perfect way to meet other people. Ask a group of friends—male and female—to go in with you to share expenses. Have each host or hostess invite five, ten, or even more people, depending on the size of your budget and the location for the party. Many garden clubs, women's clubs, and other organizations make extra money by renting out their facilities, so check around your community if your own home is too small for a crowd.

Plan your party at a slow time of the year, not around Christmas or Thanksgiving, when many people have other business and social obligations. It sometimes helps to have a theme, such as Halloween, a land-locked cruise to nowhere, or an unusual holiday such as National Pickle Week. Check in your local library for *Chase's Calendar of Events* for lists of unusual weeks. A woman we know once gave a "Come as You're Coming Back" reincarnation costume party. Use your imagination.

You can use icebreakers such as pinning part of a famous couple on each guest's back and giving prizes to those finding their famous mate, such as Caesar and Cleopatra, Tarzan and Jane, and so on. Remember, however, that many people aren't game players or at least don't think they are. Try to get them involved, but never embarrass a guest. If they see others having fun, chances are they'll give it a try to be a good sport. But if you see everyone's eyes glazing over, declare games over and bring out more snacks.

Attending Church or Synagogue

Wouldn't your mother be happy to know that you found someone special in your church or synagogue! It's a good place to begin if you're just starting to date again and you definitely want someone of your religious persuasion. Most churches and synagogues have singles groups, not only for the young singles, but also for the "mature" singles. You'll probably feel comfortable there, especially if you've been a regular attendee. But even if you attend only the social events, you'll have something in common to talk about. While you may not meet anyone that night, you may meet his or her sister or brother who is dying to play matchmaker.

Going to Conferences, Seminars, and Lectures

There are thousands of conferences, seminars, and lectures conducted in the United States every day, not to mention an equal number in countries you might like to visit. In addition to meeting people with interests similar to yours, you'll find that the subjects are as diverse as understanding tax law, environmental issues, improving your golf game, spiritual healing, and feng shui. Your local newspaper can give you details on the ones in your community. If you'd like to venture further out, try the Internet or look for articles about upcoming events in major newspapers such as the *New York Times*, the *Chicago Tribune*, the *Boston Globe*, and so on. Call the chamber of commerce or the tourist information bureau of any city you'd like to visit, and ask what conferences or seminars are being given there.

Getting into Sports

Attending sporting events and exercising are wonderful ways to meet people. Look around the gym, softball field, track, golf course, tennis court, swimming pool, or the spectator stands at the stadium or basketball arena. You don't have to be an expert in the sport. In fact, if you find someone interesting, ask questions about how to use the equipment, what does he or she think about the lineup, team's chances, or the coach.

Become a Volunteer and Find a Friend

If you've never done much volunteering, this is a good time to start. Volunteering not only makes you feel good—which is reflected through your body language, attitude, and by your conversation with those you meet—but it also is good for you physically and emotionally. A study by researchers at the University of Michigan in Ann Arbor revealed that "people who volunteered for an average of just forty hours a year (less than one hour a week) had a 30 percent lower mortality rate."

What's more, volunteering gives you the opportunity to meet others you might not otherwise know, while you help others and learn or improve your skills. A sixty-plus woman found Habitat for Humanity great fun, although she barely knew a hammer from a screwdriver. She says, "There was a lot of fresh air and a chance to learn new skills on the job. Each team had a captain who knew what she was doing and in less than half an hour, I was putting up siding and installing windows. I still point with pride to the house I helped build, even if my group first put the siding upside down. I often get together with other members of my team, none of whom I knew before I tried my hand at home building."

If building homes for those who need them doesn't sound interesting to you, think of other ways you can help others and meet interesting people at the same time. You can help in food kitchens, mentor young people who need an older person's guidance, teach reading to one of thousands who can't read, learn sign language, become a hospital volunteer, or be a docent at your local museum or art gallery. Even the smallest of towns have opportunities for volunteerism.

How to Find Organizations That Need Volunteers

By working alongside others who enjoy the same work, you'll begin to share other events and interests in your life. When you meet people who share your passionate concerns, you'll be on your way to finding the harmonious person you are looking for. Here's how to find an organization that may need your help:

- Look through your local newspaper for articles about various nonprofit groups.
- Check with your priest, minister, or rabbi for volunteer opportunities within your religious community or with additional outreach programs your organization supports.

- Listen to what others are talking about, and if the group sounds interesting, ask about becoming a volunteer.
- Stop by a local school or hospital to learn about its volunteer opportunities. Don't be insulted or concerned if you have to go through a security and background check before you're accepted. It's nothing personal, just life as it is today.
- Contact your local United Way office or learn about opportunities for volunteering in your community by checking out Volunteers of America at *www.voa.org.*
- Consider foster grandparenting or joining the Service Corps of Retired Executives (SCORE) (*www.score476.org*).
- If there's a local chapter of a national organization— American Cancer Society, American Heart Association, American Lung Association, and so on—stop by the office and ask how you can get involved.

How to Find the Right Fit

The good aspect of volunteering is that you can quit if you find the work isn't fulfilling. Even so, you should select your volunteer job as carefully as you would a paying job because you need to be interested in what you're doing and be serious about making a difference. Ask yourself the following questions:

- *Why does this group exist?* If you can't think of any reason, you probably won't feel very committed to serving it.
- *What is my motivation for donating time to this group?* If it's to find somebody special and you don't feel you're going to and you're not enjoying the work anyway, then bow out. But don't quit just because the man or woman of your dreams isn't

on the scene . . . yet. Someday your prince or princess may come, and if you love what you're doing, then have patience.

- *How can I best serve this organization?* While you may want to use your writing or artist talents or your accounting abilities, you also may prefer a change of pace and do something different. Many people drop out of an organization simply because they haven't been put into the right job slot.
- *Am I willing to take my volunteer job seriously?* The organization may depend heavily on your services. If you don't show up, you may create tremendous problems for it. Do what you've said you'll do, and if you aren't willing to, then resign.
- *Do I like the people I'll be working with?* Be honest. If you don't like kids, animals, or sick people, don't volunteer to work directly with them. You can still serve the organization in other ways. Try not to have preconceived ideas, however. You might be surprised to find that you adore mentoring a teenager when you thought you couldn't stand that age group!
- *Am I overcommitting?* It's easy to say yes to everyone as you try to meet more people, but if you find yourself running from meeting to meeting or fall into bed exhausted at night, you may need to sort through your volunteer work just as you do your closet, and get rid of what no longer works for you.
- *What are the benefits?* Sir Wilfred Thomason Grenfell, an English physician and missionary, probably put it best when he said: "The service we render to others is really the rent we pay for our room on this earth." And if you also find a special friend while you're doing so, you've been prepaid twofold.

Go Back to School

You can learn while you yearn to meet that special someone. Learn something new—in schools, seminars, or special classes. It doesn't matter whether it's a new language; a course in existentialism, Plato, or Shakespeare; knitting or quilting; a car mechanics class; or even computer technology. The people in your class will share the wonders of discovery with you—a good beginning for a lasting friendship.

Don't worry if the class is filled with students younger than yourself. Age is an artificial and arbitrary divider and it's wasteful to not encourage friendships just because the others are younger than you are. Gender doesn't (and shouldn't) play a part either. It really doesn't matter if you're an older woman with younger male friends or an older man with younger female friends. When you're enjoying another person's company, age dissipates like cotton candy in the rain.

Vivian, a fifty-year-old newly divorced woman, moved to Colorado and took some courses on Native Americans. She quickly developed an interest in Native American crafts, especially turquoise jewelry. One day she went to an art-and-craft expo and ran into—literally—a tall, exotic Native American, whom she discovered had made some of the jewelry in the show. They talked about his jewelry-making craft, went out for a coffee, and talked for hours. She still is talking with this younger man, now over the breakfast table. You can't catch fish if you don't go near the water.

Take Up Dancing—You'll Get More Than Exercise

Another woman, also newly divorced, joined a dance class. Now they're learning the tango, and she not only doesn't want for attentive partners, she also is planning a trip to South America with part of the tango group. Has she found someone special yet? No, but she's having fun and enjoying herself. What's more, all the people she's met know other people who know . . . well, you get the idea.

The plus you get when you dance is tactile—being touched. When you're alone, that's often the sense that's most deprived. Touching and being held while you're dancing obviously isn't the same as being caressed or being made love to, but until that occurs, it's a comforting substitute.

In her book, *A Gift for Healing*, Deborah Cowens, M.S.N., R.N., A.N.P., and her coauthor Tom Monte remind us that "touch is also a fundamental means of communication between people . . . The need to be touched continues through our lives. A hug, a kiss, lovemaking, and a rewarding pat on the back or shoulder—all of these are examples of how touch is used every day to communicate love, support, reconciliation, and even healing."

Helen Colton, author of *The Gift of Touch*, tells of an American woman who returned to the United States after living in France. She was asked, "What was the single difference you experienced in French life?" She answered: "The physical affection French families give each other." Colton adds: "Our discomfort [of touching] is a reflection of the still-powerful Puritan heritage that taught us to equate touching with sexuality."

That fear of touching is still with us, unfortunately, as seen by primary school teachers who hesitate hugging their young students for fear of being charged with sexual molestation or coworkers who are unwilling to even give peers a pat on the back or reassuring squeeze on the arm for fear of it being termed sexual harassment. Hugging and touching, common to many ethnic groups, are gestures unfortunately often mistaken by others. Even in the health care field, touching is often lacking as the late Norman Cousins wrote in his book, *Anatomy of an Illness*. In it he described the "utter void created by the longing—ineradicable, unremitting, pervasive—for warmth of human contact. A warm smile and an outstretched hand were valued even above the offerings of modern science, but the latter were far more accessible than the former."

Never underestimate the importance of being touched. Babies who aren't caressed actually suffer from "failure to thrive" and waste away. The same is true with elderly patients with no visitors or tactile stimulation in some nursing homes. We *all* need to be touched. Dancing is an enjoyable way to receive these special touches.

Experiment with Internet Dating Services

Explore the Internet—along with the more than 18 million people who play this "dating" game each month.

There are numerous sites to explore such as *www. personals.yahoo.com* and *www.google.com*. Type in the word "personals." There's also *http://matchmaker.com, http://senior friendfinder.com,* and *Great-Expectations.net*. Online dating can be fun, although it can be dangerous if you don't follow these simple rules:

• *Be honest about yourself and your appearance.* Don't describe yourself as thirty-five, slender, and blond if you're subtracting twenty or thirty years and pounds. After all, you two may hit it off online and you'll want to meet each other at some point; then where do you put those extra years and pounds? We stick by our "tell the truth" advice. No one likes surprises. Besides, if you're not honest to begin with and you start to see each other, it's hard to build a relationship with lies for a foundation.

• *Don't give your real name, address, or telephone number.* Keep this personal information private until you feel comfortable with the person with whom you've been "chatting."

- *Think about what you're typing in on the computer.* Be upbeat and don't complain about work, your fights with your sister, or your poor health and constant visits to the doctor. It sounds too negative. Instead, describe what activities you enjoy. Are you a hiker and biker or do you prefer strolling through art galleries and seeing plays and movies? Grabbing a hot dog and a beer at the ballgame or dining by candlelight at a French restaurant? Learning to type braille and using sign language or studying the classics?

- *Meet in a public place.* For the first few times, always meet the person in a place where you're not alone together. You can still get to know one another and you'll be a lot safer if things get strange.

- *Take your time getting to know the other person.* You should get a sense of who this new friend is before you invite him or her into your home. You need to make an assessment of this person's character and whether or not you can trust him or her.

- *Be prepared for disappointment.* Although you also can be lucky, chances are the first person you meet won't be the person of your dreams.

Play the Computer Match Game

Play the "dating game" with computer matchmaking programs. There are literally hundreds of matchmaking Web sites. A few of the more popular sites include Match.com, Matchmaker.com, Yahoo.com, digitalcity.com, and ThirdAge.com, the last being a Web site primarily for baby boomers and older. You can also go to your search engine and type in "online dating services."

With many of these programs, interested individuals create a videotape, telling about their interests and backgrounds along with what they are looking for in another person. You can include such requests as "nonsmokers," a specific religion or ethnicity, geographic area, and even get as specific as height and hair color. Sometimes, each individual just fills out an interest form. Then you select those you'd like to meet and see if that person also wants to meet with you. We know of many cases where those couples "clicked" and eventually married.

Although some of these matchmaking services are free, fees on some Web sites may range from $20 a month and upward. Be sure you understand the fee structure before committing yourself to a membership.

Take Out a Personal Ad in Newspapers and Magazines

As with the computer dating services, personal ads (often known as "friendship" ads) can help you meet new and interesting people. Be careful, though, not to give your address right away, and if you decide to meet each other, do so in a public place for the first couple of times until you feel comfortable and safe.

Most personal ads use abbreviations to denote married or divorced, Christian or Jewish, smoker or nonsmoker, and so on. For example, you'll see abbreviations such as M for married, D for divorced, C for Christian, J for Jewish, N/S for nonsmoker, and N/D for nondrinker. You'll catch on quickly. The ads usually read something like:

> *DWF, 58, HWP, ISO friend companion, LTR.*
> *Loves fishing, flea markets, gardening, beach*
> *trips, and cooking.*

The first part of the ad can be decoded as this: Divorced, white, female, 58 years old, height and weight are in proportion, in search of a friend and companion for a long-term relationship. This may seem like studying a foreign language, but you'll catch on quickly. After all, in this course, the results could really win you a prize.

Rekindle Former Friendships

You've probably heard of a couple who had known each other in high school, married other people, then years later divorced or were widowed, looked up the former friendship and rekindled the friendship, which then turned into love and finally marriage. It does happen and often. So don't throw away your invitation to your high school or college reunion. And don't fret that you're heavier than you were, have less hair, or have too many wrinkles. So will the other attendees. Go there and become reacquainted with those you enjoyed knowing years ago. Catch up on their lives. If you enjoyed their company years ago, you may be surprised to find you still have a few sparks.

You also can find former friends through the Internet or by contacting your high school or college alumni center. They have paid staff whose job it is to keep track of everyone (and hopefully, get donations from them).

Let Your Friends and Family Play Matchmaker

Almost everyone wants to play matchmaker to his or her friends or relatives. There's a special feeling when you can claim, "I put them together" or "I knew they'd be right for each other."

Sam, widowed at age fifty-nine, said his friends were interested in fixing him up whenever he was ready. "I wasn't really prepared to start dating, but although I was still working, weekends and evenings were so lonely that when they called, I agreed to go to their home to meet a woman they knew. Then the four of us went out together. It didn't seem as much of a date that way, because I was still feeling somewhat disloyal about seeing another woman, although my wife had been gone for six months. I had a lot of guilt associated with the whole process [of dating]. Whether it made sense or not isn't important. It was there." Later, he and the woman in question were married.

Ellen met her husband on a blind date, but not with him. She was actually fixed up with one of her husband's friends who had come in from out of town for a party. The inadvertent matchmaker in this case was Ellen's husband's girlfriend, who was just trying to be helpful by finding dates for his friends. She didn't realize that she was accidentally selecting her successor.

Dean was divorced after twenty-seven years of marriage and two children. He dated on and off for the next five years, without finding anyone special. One summer he went to Florida to visit his sister, Betty. "I'd like to find someone special," he admitted. "But I just haven't found anyone I like, let alone love." After he returned to his apartment up north, Betty mentioned to her girlfriend, Mary Anne, that her brother, Dean, had been visiting. "Why didn't you introduce me?" asked Mary Anne. "You know I've been looking for someone to go out with?" Betty confessed she hadn't even thought of fixing up her brother with her friend because they lived in two different states in different parts of the country. Nevertheless, she suggested, "Why don't you e-mail him? You can become pen pals!" The two women laughed at the idea, but Mary Anne took Dean's e-mail address and wrote to him.

A few days later, Dean e-mailed her back. That began a fairly steady exchange of e-mails back and forth as Dean and

Mary Anne got to know more about each other. She went up north to visit him and he came back to Florida to spend time with her. They continued to date by e-mail, and eventually got engaged. Now they're married.

The moral? Tell your friends and relatives just what you're looking for. A companion who enjoys skiing, tennis, and other outdoor sports? A friend to join you for dinner, dancing, theater, and perhaps travel? Or just someone with whom you can go out to lunch or dinner? Don't limit yourself by being too specific, though. Don't expect immediate satisfaction, although you may be pleasantly surprised. Let them all scramble to be the first to say, "I made the match!"

When You Find a New Friend, Don't Lose Yourself

Be on guard for hints of control battles. Although it may seem nice for a change to have someone take charge, deciding where to go for dinner, what activities will follow, what movies to see, what you should wear, and so on, you may be getting subtle clues that this person needs to be in control. There's really no room in a friendship (and a potentially budding relationship) for a battle for control. A condition of friendship is the letting go of power over another.

You may remember back in elementary school when you had a "best" friend. Everything went well as long as you agreed with your friend. But when you didn't and he or she attempted to control you, the friendship was finished. Abuse of power can end not only traditional friendships, but also love relationships, which should have true friendship at their center.

When we were in high school and college, we remember complaining about some of our peers who dumped their other friends as soon as they had a boyfriend or girlfriend.

Unfortunately, older people may be just as guilty of doing the same thing.

"He doesn't like me to spend time with my friends," complained one woman in her sixties. "He gets jealous. He says it's because he cares for me and wants to spend all his time with me. At first, it was flattering. but now . . ." Contrary to what you may think, this type of jealousy does not prove the other's deep love; instead, it is a form of control. When you try to regulate who another person may or may not see, you are keeping a relationship from growing and developing. Possessiveness poisons.

When You Find a New Friend, Keep Your Old Ones, Too

When you're in your fifties, sixties, or more, you've obviously lived a lot of years, and unless you've been held in solitary confinement, you've met a great many people, many of whom, we hope, are still friends. While the hope is that the new person in your life will like those individuals you've grown close to over the years, that doesn't always happen. But just because your significant other's personality doesn't mesh as well as you'd like with your friends, that doesn't mean you can't be friends with those from your past.

Of course you're caught up with the emotion of finding someone special and you want to spend all your time with that individual. But it's important to save a little time for your other buddies, too. Plan lunch dates, "girls' night out," "men's poker club," or just an occasional getaway with the old gang.

In a healthy relationship, there is space for each person to enjoy his or her individuality. While you may enjoy each other's company and consider each other best friends, there are times when you need to be with other close old friends or engage in favored activities with others. That's why it's said, "Make new friends but keep the old; one is silver, one is gold." This is especially true for couples who are fully retired and spend a great deal of time together. You need to widen the circle to let other friends in. Hopefully, the person you feel closest to is comfortable in allowing you that space, knowing full well that it is only through having some space that people and relationships can grow and thrive.

Chapter 7

The Masculine Mystique

"If a woman wears gay colors, rouge, and a startling hat, a man hesitates to take her out. If she wears a little turban and a tailored suit, he takes her out and stares all evening at a woman in gay colors and a startling hat."

—*Baltimore Beacon*

THE TRUTHFULNESS OF this quote, written in yesteryear, is still timely. We all know that Freud once said: "Women! What do they want?" But history hasn't recorded what Mrs. Freud said. It was: "Men! When they're single—no matter what their age—they still wonder what's missing in their lives, but are afraid to commit."

Men's Roles Are Being Refined

We consider that one element of the hesitation today is the refined definition of men's lives. In part, the transformation of what is generally considered to be a man's role is a positive slide to the middle. The new family today holds more promise than its traditional predecessor, mainly due to the influence exerted by women's "liberation." We see the new family as a healthy, exciting, and enriching opportunity for both men and women, one that will, in redefining family life as well, prevent it from self-destructing. But if you are reentering the dating arena with an eye to possible marriage, especially if you've been out of the single scene for some years and most especially if you are a man, you need to be aware of these changes.

Some men still resist—some loudly and some more subtly—the legitimate demands of an increasingly large number of women who simply want equal opportunity in decision-making, career choice, and leisure-time activities, as well as equal pay for equal work. But fortunately, a growing number of men support these claims as only right in today's world. Men hoping to compete in befriending and possibly snaring one of these enlightened women need to understand and accept the motive behind these needs. It is not, as some would claim, a "them against us" mentality, but rather the only way to create a "we."

In her new introduction to *The Feminine Mystique* (2001), entitled "Metamorphosis—Two Generations Later," Betty Friedan wrote: "It's the men who have to break through to a new way of thinking about themselves and society."

In the movie *Down with Love,* the heroine is made famous by the publication of her nonfiction book that tells women they no longer need marriage to be successful. That certainly rings true today as the number of women in law school outnumbers the men. Many medical school first-year classes are equal between the genders and some have more women than men. There are medical practices where all the partners are women, major companies where the CEOs are women, women who own businesses, women who make favorable deals on new cars, and women who ask men out on dates. It is a changed world and equality is its name.

If you're planning to jump into and establish this type of egalitarian relationship, whether just dating regularly, moving in together, or marrying, you need to realize that a couple must enjoy open, honest communication and mutual respect, with each supporting the other's talents while allowing, without reservation, any imperfections. This is the only way each partner can really develop to his or her fullest potential. Perhaps Steven Carter and Julia Sokol said it best when they wrote in their book *Men Like Women Who Like Themselves*: "Treat a man like he's a creature from another planet, and he'll act like a creature from another planet." We embrace this thinking as we do the concept of the egalitarian relationship, which both of us enjoy with our respective partners.

Thankfully, most men no longer feel threatened by an egalitarian relationship and now share the housework (and childcare, if any). If you have married, grown sons, you may be amazed at how much your son helps with the housework, shopping, and, if there are children, the child care. What men do today may be vastly different from the chores performed by their fathers, and without realizing it, you (male or female) may overtly wonder at the merging of what used to be considered "gender roles."

There is a wonderful story about a woman who was asked how her married daughter was getting along. "Oh," the woman replied. "She is so lucky. Her husband feeds and bathes the children, grocery shops and cooks dinner, baby-sits so she can work out at the gym, and takes the kids to Disney World so she can have a day to herself. And how's your son?" The other woman shook her head. "My son isn't so lucky. He married a very demanding woman. He has to feed and bathe the children, grocery shop and cook dinner, baby-sit so she can work out at the gym, and take the kids to Disney World so she can have a day to herself."

The moral of this? Not only is equality in the eye of the beholder, but also, don't judge the relationships of others. What might not work for you may work perfectly for others. Try to be flexible. As you must know, the times are no longer changing—

they have changed. When you go back into the dating world—especially if it's been awhile—you may find there are rippling effects on your world as well.

Over the forty-two years that one woman has been married, she admits there have been subtle changes in the way chores are divided between her and her husband. "My husband always enjoyed grocery shopping, so he'll often pop in to pick up things for dinner, now that there's just the two of us. He also takes the sheets and shirts to the dry cleaners and picks them up. I arrange for repair needs around the condo and make sure the air conditioning filters are changed. I cook, he clears, and I clean up. We make the bed together and so on. There wasn't a great discussion about who does what. We just took those chores we preferred. I'm also in charge of reducing clutter, and although I do a lousy job of it, he doesn't seem to mind enough to take that chore over."

Today, there is ample evidence of the excitement, joy, and power of family life. Couples who marry do so not for social status, economic reasons, escape, sex, or pregnancy, but because they truly care about each other and respect each other as equals. They spend time having fun together and also are becoming aware that religion is not a burden but rather an affirmation of the spirit that brings comfort, joy, and relaxation to a hectic, complex life. They enjoy being together, having fun, making decisions, and talking about everything from daily mundane events to philosophical and religious issues. Religion plays an increasingly important part in many of their lives as they find it brings a sense of peace and comfort in their hectic and complex lives.

According to "Contemporary Marriage" in *The New Handbook of Psychotherapy and Counseling with Men*, authors L. Gilbert and S. Walker wrote that studies of relationships found that in the last two decades, both men's and women's expectations have changed significantly and become less rigid. Today, partners in happy, long-term relationships are three times more likely to embrace a flexible definition of women's and men's roles.

How to Ride the New Wave

Although change comes with some difficulty as we grow older, this sense of equality is a healthy and welcome change. It may seem strange at first as you explore a new relationship in later life, but you'll quickly learn that there's more time for fun and relaxation when two share the load, without keeping track of whose job it is to pay for lunch, grocery shop, fill the car with gas, change lightbulbs, or empty the dishwasher.

What does this mean if you're male? It means you shouldn't worry about available partners. There are many more single women than men, a fact of which women are well aware. (If you're gay and prefer male partners, turn to Chapter 15.) It also means that you're going to have to allow your "sensitive side" to come out of hiding and tear up your father's job description of "how to be a real man." Terrance Real, in the December 2002 issue of *Psychotherapy Networker,* suggests that men are just not raised to be "intimate partners, but to be strong, competitive performers." Real proposes an even more important idea: "Men aren't afraid of intimacy; they are afraid of subjection." He adds: "Many men read emotional receptivity as an invitation to be run over. The pressure to be hard, logical, independent, and stoic all too often sets men up to be emotionally distant, arrogant, numb to their own feelings, and unconcerned about everyone else's, as well as contemptuous of vulnerability and weakness."

If you recognize these characteristics within yourself, we propose that you follow the basic philosophy of this book, which is to look for a friend first, not a lifetime romance. Test your capacity to become your true self and a close and intimate friend. If you want to spend time with someone, but you are still afraid to make a commitment, remember that there is no need to ever consider marriage. You can always live together and see what happens. But remember what Aristotle said about friendship: "Wishing to be friends is quick work, but friendship is a slow-ripening fruit" (*Nicomachean Ethics*). Perhaps it's best to be reminded of author and philosopher Elie Wiesel's perception: "Friendship marks a life even more deeply than love. Love risks degenerating into obsession, friendship is never anything but sharing" (*The Gates of the Forest*, 1966).

Don't be jaded by authors who, while acknowledging the problem of men's inability to commit, ascribe it to women being less willing to limit their ambitions to make life more comfortable for the men in their lives. If you're afraid of equality in a relationship and think you can escape it, you're probably living in the past. Today, the best relationships are egalitarian. So go for it. Look for the women who love life, and perhaps, if you're lucky, they'll love you as well. If you still feel stuck in the mid-twentieth century, read books by Terrance Real, such as *How Can I Get Through to You?* and *I Don't Want to Talk about It*, or visit his Web site at *www.terryreal.com*.

Are There Natural Differences Between Men and Women?

If there are differences between men and women, then love can flourish only when both parties respect these differences. "Natural" differences may not be entirely correct, but it is true that cultural and societal forces determine the main behavioral and psychological differences between men and women, especially how our parents raised us. It's what Dorian Solot and

Marshall Miller call "tribal differences" in their book *Unmarried to Each Other*. You'll read more about these tribal differences in Chapter 13. But as these differences are environmental, not natural, these forces can be reshaped and changed.

Many of us have been exposed to simplistic ideas of compromise regarding the maintaining of relationships that are not likely to have been sound in the first place. Married partners, for example, often attempt to stay together to preserve family unity. For the sake of the children, the couple will develop all kinds of compromises to stay married. Such arrangements do not necessarily make a good marriage or bring happiness to anyone. On the other hand, sometimes a compromise can be good because the result might be far better than the consequences of a disastrous divorce. Learning to compromise and negotiate can be beneficial to any type of relationship—friendship, romantic, or marriage.

You also may have absorbed stereotypical notions about those who act "just like a woman" or "just like a man" from your own family and, without realizing it, carry it into your present or future relationship. This view is a kind of avoidance, often representing ways of covering up basic personality flaws. Beware of such stereotypes. It isn't helpful to avoid addressing crucial issues by dismissing them, saying, "all men are like this" or "all women are like that." A resignation, which is a kind of despair, can set in, and it becomes all too easy to give up on trying to change a bad or troublesome situation. It is much better to operate in terms of conflict resolution, while remembering that not all conflicts really need to be resolved. Some tension and differences of opinion exist in even the best relationships. In an egalitarian partnership, differences between sexes enhance, rather than detract from, the relationship.

The best approach is to find legitimate, workable compromises that satisfy both partners in a relationship. Don't expect to solve every problem. As philosopher William James observed: "Wisdom is learning what to overlook."

Checkup for Relationship Health

Pat Love, Ed.D., of the Austin Family Institute and author of *Truth About Love* offers this Relationship Inventory Test for you to score yourself to see your perception of what makes a good relationship. According to research, which of the following statements are predictors of relationship happiness and stability? Put a check mark by the statements you believe are predictors:

1. Resolving problems ....❒
2. Both partners heeding one another's advice ....❒
3. Equality between the spouses..................................❒
4. Money ....❒
5. Good sex life ....❒
6. Couple having good friends ....❒
7. Love..❒
8. Being good friends...❒
9. Making the relationship a priority..............................❒

If you checked 2, 4, 6, 8, and 9, you're absolutely correct.

You may wonder why the other points fail to be good predictors of relationship happiness and stability:

No. 1: Many problems are never solved and often, really, don't need to be. Friendship, as well as with good relationships, are never exactly equal. They are fluid, shifting first in one's favor, then the other. The secret to their success is that they never constantly topple in one direction.

No. 3: Exact equality can lead to score keeping and statements such as "You always . . ." and "You never . . ."

No. 5: A good sex life isn't a definite predictor of relationship happiness and stability. There are very happy and stable relationships in which, for varying reasons, there is no actual sexual intercourse. There are, however, other forms of intimacy.

No. 7: Feelings of love vary over the lifetime of a relationship, so it really isn't a predictor of what makes a good relationship. Being good friends is.

Chapter 8

Why Worry About Age?

"There is a fountain of youth; it is your mind, your talents, the creativity you bring to your life and the lives of people you love. When you learn to tap this source, you will truly have defeated age."

—Sophia Loren, actress

PERHAPS AMERICAN ACTRESS Billie Burke said it best: "Age is something that doesn't matter unless you are a cheese." And yet, most of us spend far too much time agonizing over our age and what we "should" do because of those years. Are we too old to look for someone new? What if he or she is "too young"? Should we "act our age"? If so, what exactly is that? Rocking in the old rocker? Snoozing in front of the television set? Standing on the sidelines, watching the "younger folk" having fun? What constitutes "appropriate age" behavior?

Age-appropriate activities are whatever you want them to be, whatever you enjoy, and what you find a way to do even if you have certain physical limitations. But age—a number representing the actual years you have lived—should not be the determining factor. There are many older couples who enjoy playing basketball, tennis, skiing, flying airplanes, weight lifting, jogging, speed walking, dancing, and a myriad of other activities, including frequent sex.

Differences in Age Are Just Numbers

So many people get hung up on age when they reenter the dating world, as though there were certain rules one had to conform to, such as the man being older than the woman or the woman not being too much younger than the man. We're human beings, not fine wine, so age really isn't that important.

Vivian, a divorcee, is dating a man fifteen years younger than she is. She says, "Ted calls me four to five times a day to tell me he loves me and misses me. The fact is, I love my freedom and the time I spend doing Vivian things . . . but I also cherish the time we can be together. We laugh a lot and, of course, are still finding out about each other. I know we come from different backgrounds, but at my age [50s] I find that fascinating. I don't have time to think about what others think. I just want to feel joyful, loved, appreciated, treated with respect. I want to laugh and have fun. And that's what I'm feeling. I'm experiencing a love and intimacy I've never before experienced."

Carol is married to a man eight years older than she is. "The only time I've ever noticed any difference," she reports, "is when he talks about movie stars I've never heard of. No one ever thinks anything is odd about my husband being eight years older. Now, if *I* were eight years older than he is, I'm sure there would be a lot of conversation." And there would be, even though society's "rules" about age restrictions seem to be weakening, possibly because some of the female diehards have found younger men for themselves. The only problems we see that may come up are not in the compatibility arena, but rather in the physical world when signs of aging appear and become chronic and/or debilitating. But, as one man said, "The older one gets, the less important age becomes. There's less difference between people ages fifty and seventy than there is between twenty and forty. And as for any concern that one day the younger person possibly might have to care for the older one, well, would you pass up a wonderful relationship because of what might happen? I wouldn't and didn't."

The *New York Times* has a section entitled "Sunday Styles," where classy people, including gays and lesbians, announce their weddings or commitment ceremonies. Most of the marriages are of people in their late twenties and early thirties. But we've been encouraged by some of the nuptials for older couples. Most of the individuals have been previously married. Take a look at some of the couples:

> *Bride 41, groom 43 (They've lived together for seventeen years and are now planning to marry.)*
> *Bride 66, groom 64*
> *Bride 42 (divorced), groom 40 (widower)*
> *Bride 55, groom 66*
> *Bride 72, groom 68*
> *Bride 50, groom 50 (She'll keep her name.)*
> *Bride 56 (widow), groom 59*
> *Bride 68 (divorced), groom 72 (widower)*
> *Groom 49, groom 33 (a commitment ceremony)*

One name of a new bride you're sure to recognize is that of actress Carol Channing, age eighty-two, who married her junior high school sweetheart who is eighty-three years old. Another, feminist Gloria Steinem, took advantage of a woman's right to change her mind. After saying she would never marry, she did, and at age sixty-six. So you can see, there's no reason to be concerned about the age factor. Actually, for women, life seems to get better at age fifty. A survey of 200 "fifty-something" women found that two-thirds of them were happier after their menopause. Sixty-six percent were more independent, 64 percent said their sex lives had improved or not changed, and 59 percent said personal and family relationships had gotten better.

In *The Fountain of Age*, Betty Friedan urges her readers to "be open to the new possibilities of living." And there are so many of them. Life today is far different from that of our parents and grandparents. Life span is increased, while age restrictions have burst like the record for the four-minute mile. So never say, "I'm too old."

Not Every Couple Wants to Marry

Remember that companionship, not necessarily marriage, is the goal of many people looking for love again. An illuminating article in the *Los Angeles Times* (March 18, 2003) titled "At Long Last Love: Seniors Find Relationships More Golden Than They Ever Dreamed" detailed an array of successful couplings of people over sixty-five. Guess it was news to them, but not to us. The Census Bureau's most current survey (2000) found that more older Americans than ever—approximately 112,000, ages sixty-five and older—are coupling up (and hundreds more probably are, but didn't want to admit it, certainly not to the federal government). That is up 60 percent from 1990. Seniors are cohabiting more often than marrying for a host of reasons, including alimony, social security, taxes, and problems relating to inheritance.

Why is this happening? We'd like to answer: "Because they can." But there are other underlying reasons. People are living longer and are healthier and more active than in the past. The average life span rose from 77 years to 77.2 years in 2001. The prevailing wisdom is becoming, if being alone is not your preference, why not enjoy your life by doing something about it? Don't limit yourself by worrying if you're too old to start dating again or, if you're a woman, by disqualifying yourself from a prospective relationship because the man is younger than you. Age is in the mind.

A 2001 study by Bumpass and Sweet entitled "Marriage, Divorce, and Intergenerational Relationships" revealed that "while sixty-three percent of couples who live together think marriage would significantly change their relationship, levels of commitment, supportiveness, and sharing once exclusively seen among married people are now just as common among those living together."

While we encourage people to profit from mistakes and good experiences from previous marriages, there are issues that are unique to a new coupling. These actual life histories illustrate some of them.

Susan and Al are now in their seventies. Both were widowed and discovered each other through an Internet dating service. They became best friends, then fell in love as they had never experienced before, and yet they decided not to marry. Both lived comfortably in well-established homes (fortunately, not too far from each other), and both wanted to keep their residences, mainly because of their families. Their children and grandchildren adored the memories of their parents and grandparents in the context of a home they considered precious (and to be honest, there were also questions of inheritance, not discussed, but understood). Thus, this loving couple coupled and enjoyed their intimate relationship without actually living together. Susan and Al had joyful comments about their newly found love. "If you experienced love when you were young, you are going to want to replicate that feeling when you are older . . . Life is short. Don't waste a second of it being miserable or unhappy."

We know of other older couples who decided to marry, but felt that a prenuptial agreement was necessary to ensure an inheritance for the grandchildren. Sam, for example, remarried at age seventy to a widow age sixty-five, three years after his wife had died. For his remaining five years of life, he appeared to be happier than any time in his life. His three adult children observed with awe and joy a renewed man. "Don't misunderstand me," his son reflected. "My mother was a good woman and mother, but 'miracles' do happen. The Talmud says, 'Expect miracles, but don't count on them.'"

Jack and Sarah are another couple who decided not to marry. After knowing each other and dating for a few years, Jack moved into Sarah's well-established home. He agreed to pay rent and share expenses. Their income and bank accounts are individually managed. It works for them.

Ethel and her partner are yet another example. Ethel was widowed twenty years ago. Living in New York City, she dated infrequently, but her life was mainly enhanced by making good friends with other single women, enjoying the cultural opportunities in Manhattan and taking care of her three children (now adults) with children of their own. At age seventy-seven, still healthy and full of energy, she moved to the Boston area to be near one of her children. She met a recently widowed man of seventy-five at the local synagogue. They became best friends. For pertinent reasons, they decided not to live together, but spend most of their time enjoying each other's company.

Marrying and signing a prenuptial agreement, or not marrying and living in separate quarters, are just two options. There are many variations that each couple needs to work out to both person's satisfaction. Should you worry about age differences? Not really. What difference does it really make? If you are in search of a friend and not a storybook romance, then age is seldom the issue—health and vitality are. There are sixty- and seventy-year-olds who are more alive, more full of zip and vigor, with more enthusiasm and more involvement in active sports than many forty- and fifty-year-olds you may know. Some of the best partnerships we know about have unusual age discrepancies. For example, one of my (Sol's) closest couple friends includes a thirty-five-year-old man who is married to a fifty-one-year-old woman with two adult children. Both were very active in a religious mission. They've been married for fifteen years now and are still joyfully partnered with no regrets. Many of the best partnerships do have unusual age discrepancies.

Don't let your age get in the way. The March 31, 2003 issue of *New York Magazine* had in its "Strictly Personals" column an ad from a "mensch" in his sixties looking for a fit woman with wit; an ad from a woman looking for a man in his fifties or sixties; an ad from a slim fifty-five-year-old looking for a fifty-five to sixty-eight-year-old gentleman nonsmoker; and an ad from a cultured woman looking for a fifty-five to sixty-five-year-old man for "friendship and romance." You're not alone, as these personal ads illustrate.

As we've followed these personal ad columns over time, we've noted that more and more singles are looking for companionship and friendship (and nonsmokers!). But it is interesting to note, the majority of the wish lists still focus on the adjectives "attractive," "slim," "great body," and the telling plea, "photo please." To which we reply, "Good luck."

Our gold award goes to the champion personal ad writer who wrote this: "Seeking woman who will allow me to be myself." You go, guy.

Being Realistic About Health Issues

In *The Johns Hopkins Medical Guide to Health After 50*, surveys conducted by the MacArthur Foundation are encouraging because they report "no significant physical or mental disabilities

are reported by 89 percent of those between 65 and 74, 73 percent of those between 75 and 84, and 40 percent of those over
age 85." That's the good news. The reality, of course, is that as
we age, most of us do develop some type of physical problems.
It may be nothing more than a little stiffness in the morning,
some acid reflux after a large meal, or high blood pressure that
needs treatment. While some illnesses can be prevented by
making wise lifestyle decisions—exercising, maintaining a
healthy diet and weight, learning to handle stress, and not
smoking—other diseases, such as cancer, heart disease, and diabetes may be more difficult to prevent, although they are usually
treatable.

Regardless who is older—the man or the woman—the
younger partner needs to be aware of potential future health
problems in the older partner. If the relationship develops into
something long-term, the chances may increase that the younger
partner could eventually become a caregiver. But many younger
members of a relationship often find that they, themselves, are
the ones developing a chronic illness and that they need to be
cared for by the older partner. That's what the marriage (and
coupling) vows mean when they say, "For better or for worse; in
sickness and in health."

There also are physical changes that arise as we age that
pertain to sexual intimacy. As men age, their testosterone levels
decrease along with their sexual potency. What's more,
according to an article by Josh Fischman in *U.S. News & World
Report,* "one study of 850 men over age 50 showed the lower
[their] hormone levels, the higher their scores on a depression
test." Impotency (also known as erectile dysfunction or ED)
afflicts an estimated 20 million American men. While 75 percent
of all cases have a medical basis—nerve disorders caused by diabetes, Parkinson's disease, multiple sclerosis, or specific surgery;
vascular problems caused by narrowing of the arteries; and

medications such as those prescribed for high blood pressure, heart disease, and allergies—impotency also can be caused by too much alcohol intake, smoking, and in some cases, it has a psychological component. Fortunately, there are treatments that may work for impotency including Viagra if their physician approves it, a vacuum device, vasodilators, or implant surgery.

Postmenopausal women also have potential sexual difficulties. The lack of estrogen may make the vaginal wall thin out and become dry, causing intercourse to be painful. Fortunately, there are a number of lubrication products available to replace the natural secretions. In addition, postmenopausal women may find their sexual desire somewhat diminished along with their ability to achieve an orgasm. It also may take longer for them to reach an orgasm, which can cause frustration for both partners.

But don't just throw in the towel, figuring you're "too old" for sexual intimacy. Keep hugging, cuddling, stroking, and otherwise staying physically close, even if it takes time for actual intercourse to take place. Talk to each other about your sexual relationship and how you can improve it, making it fun and pleasurable for you both. These are subjects that need to be discussed in any relationship, but especially in relationships where there is an age difference, so that one partner doesn't consider sexual dysfunction to be a sign of lack of sexual desire for him or her or that the older partner pulls away emotionally, becoming depressed and considers himself or herself to be a failure "that way." Sex is an important part of life no matter your age. Never let embarrassment keep you from discussing your needs or problems with your partner or getting medical help if that's needed. Be sure to read Chapter 11 for more on sexuality.

Chapter 9

The Otherwise
Perfect Person (OPP)

"Who seeks a faultless friend remain friendless."

—Turkish proverb

IT'S HARD ENOUGH STEPPING OUT into the world of dating again without handicapping yourself by setting your sights only on a "perfect" specimen of a man or woman, the ideal you've conjured up, vowing either to do better than last time or to find someone just like the person you loved and lost. Whichever way, you're creating unnecessary blockades in your path to finding a new special friend, companion, or lover. Author Edna Ferber declared: "Living in the past is a dull and lonely business; looking back strains the neck muscles, causes you to bump into people not going your way."

So forge ahead, looking not for the perfect person, but rather someone you enjoy being with and who makes you feel happy and comforts you when you're not. Saint Ailred of Rievaulx wrote: "No medicine is more valuable, none more efficacious, none better suited to the cure of all our temporal ills than a friend to whom we may turn for consolation in time of trouble, and with whom we may share our happiness in time of joy."

It's All about Making Choices

Trudy met a truly terrific man at her play-reading group. They went out for coffee afterward, and she discovered he shared many of her interests—art, literature, hiking, foreign films, and good food and wine. It sounds like a match made in heaven . . . until he lit the match and Trudy realized she had met a *smoker.* Trudy had little tolerance for being in the presence of a smoker, especially since her late husband had died from the effects of emphysema, brought on by smoking. She hated the smell and couldn't understand why today, knowing all of the dangers, people still smoke. Trudy had three options:

1. Lecture to the otherwise perfect person (OPP), describing all of the risks smoking causes, the costs, and so on
2. Say good-bye to this OPP
3. Initially deal only with her problem by asking the otherwise perfect person if he would mind not smoking in her presence

Obviously, no. 3 works best for Trudy because she gives the relationship a chance to develop before calling it quits. If OPP wants Trudy's friendship, there's a good chance that he will, at first, not smoke in her presence. If the relationship continues, the OPP could attempt (with Trudy's encouragement) to quit smoking. It would be important, however, for Trudy to understand that smoking is an addiction, and most people who smoke find it very difficult, although not impossible, to quit. Many people quit several times before being successful and some never are.

Harvey enjoyed being with MaryAnne other than the fact that she easily became inebriated after one or two drinks. Harvey could handle the situation by saying . . .

1. "I think you're great to be with, but I can't risk letting you drive home after you've had a couple of drinks. I care too much about you. Will you let me drive you home instead?"
2. "We'll have to call it quits. It embarrasses me to be with a woman who can't hold her liquor."
3. "Here's some information about AA. Call me when you can remain sober."

No. 1 works best in this situation. If Harvey really finds MaryAnne an OPP, then perhaps he can plan dates where alcoholic beverages aren't so available (such as the movies, museums, or theater) and when going out to dinner, refrain from having a drink as well.

The ultimate solution to Trudy's and Harvey's problems, of course, will come when each of their OPPs cares enough about Trudy and Harvey to make the sacrifice of giving up smoking and drinking for their sake (and the OPP's as well). If you're in a similar spot, you can urge the person you care about to join Alcoholics Anonymous, but the decision to do so and the will to continue going to meetings and to remain sober must be that person's decision. If someone else's drinking troubles you, Al-Anon can help. Call 1-888-AL-ANON (425-2666). Remember, however, that excessive alcohol consumption is bound to weaken and threaten the stability of your relationship.

Smoking and drinking are often symptoms of stress. We need to relieve stress, and the best way to do that is to solve the problems that created the stress in the first place. People can change habits, no matter how ingrained the habit may be. So you can help by allowing that person to talk out how the habit began and what stresses it masks. You can't always count on being successful, but you need to decide early on whether it's worth it to you to try. In the long run, the person you care about may require professional help and will certainly need a strong will to overcome any type of addiction—smoking, alcohol, drugs, or gambling. Be careful not to become an enabler, making excuses for this otherwise perfect person's addiction.

You both can experiment with other techniques for handling stress, such as exercising together by walking, jogging, or biking; practicing yoga or tai chi; meditating; and laughing. Yes, laughter is a wonderful stress buster and actually has many healing properties. The importance of laughter is the theme of the World Laughter Tour, a group of health care professionals who oversee more than 100 clubs across the United States and Canada where people meet to take part in "laughter exercise workouts." If you're interested, call 1-800-669-5233 (6140855-4733 international) or go online at *www.laughterclubs.com.* You may find that you and your almost perfect person have different senses of humor. You may chortle at slapstick while he or she chuckles at Jay Leno. No matter. The important trait is that you both enjoy humor as long as it isn't hurtful to another.

What if everything seems to be going well and you both enjoy your volunteer work at a center that feeds the homeless, but . . . ah, there's always that "but." The problem is that you seem to have frequent arguments. Your almost perfect partner says, "Why didn't you call if you were running late?" and you respond with, "Why do you always make nasty ethnic remarks?" Each attack stimulates more counterattacks and finally you're almost up to the "So's your old mother!" comments. Stop and listen to what you're both saying. The best way to handle these conflict situations is to use "I" messages, such as "I feel bad when you . . ." or "It depresses me when . . ." and "I know you don't realize how much it hurts me when . . ."

If the conflict's relatively unimportant, follow the philosophy of Jennie Jerome Churchill, mother of Sir Winston Churchill, the prime minister of Great Britain during World War

II, who suggested that you should "treat your friends as you do your pictures, and place them in their best light." If this advice doesn't improve the situation, perhaps this relationship isn't for you.

Obviously, if the otherwise perfect person is physically, emotionally, or verbally abusive, don't try to ignore the problem or figure it's your fault for getting the person angry. Being abusive is not a way for people to show they really care for someone else. Say a fast good-bye. Do the same for someone who abuses drugs or who has a severe drinking problem. Both could create a potential danger to you.

But problems also arise even without addictions. Rose met an OPP at a ski club meeting. George was an ardent skier, as she was, and he loved to cook, as she did. While he was not the tall, dark, and handsome man of her dreams—he was short, thin, and had red hair—that was not the problem. Rose's OPP was widowed and had two teenage daughters, and they were the problem. The girls resented Rose, resented their dad's attention to Rose, and even resented Rose trying to cook for them. Rose's choice were these:

1. Continue to try to win the girls over
2. Dump George because she really disliked his kids as much as they disliked her
3. Ignore the situation and enjoy her time with George with no expectations of some type of a future together as husband and wife

Rose gave up trying to win the girls over and instead chose no. 3. She has fun with George, enjoys the relationship, and doesn't look too far into the future.

Claudia was widowed and in her late seventies when she met Alan, a college professor in his early sixties. She hadn't expected to find love at this point in her life, but enjoyed being with Alan. They laughed a lot, dined at the best restaurants, and traveled together. Both of them had grown children and grand-children who, although not delighted with the situation, at least were pleasant to their parent's choice of a partner. When Alan suggested that he and Claudia get married, she hesitated. Her options were to . . .

1. Continue dating as they had been without marriage in the picture.
2. Listen to the concerns of her grown children who wor-ried about the age difference.
3. Decide that when happiness comes her way, she should grab it.

Claudia hesitated no longer and agreed to marry Alan. They married and he moved into her home. Claudia admits she feels years younger and is filled with energy to experience new things together with her husband.

What to Do If Your OPP Is Married

Here's a tougher problem. You work together and see each other every weekday. He's very fond of you and you of him. But he's married. You coffee and lunch together and he reveals his dissatisfaction with his marriage. He is clearly more open with you than with his wife. You are single, perhaps divorced. There's no sex now, but he is hinting at it. But you know full well that infidelity doesn't always mean sex. He has made it clear that he won't divorce his wife because he still has three children at home and doesn't want to hurt them.

You might suggest he read the book by Shirley Glass, *Not*

Just Friends: Protect Your Relationship from Infidelity and Heal the Trauma of Betrayal. Continuing with this type of relationship will almost certainly bring you heartache, no matter how perfect you think he may be for you. And you'll be missing out on the best parts of being a couple—you'll still be alone on weekends and holidays. We know it's flattering that he wants you and it's boosted your self-esteem. You feel young and in love again. But even someone who seems great from almost every other point of view may not be good for you because of the circumstances. He's married and doesn't plan to divorce.

What to Do If Your OPP Can't Get Over the Past

Another serious problem arises when someone you care about is still preoccupied with a past traumatic event. She could have been raped. He could have been sexually or physically abused as a child. Any number of situations of trauma or abuse can still be a factor in the lives of adults. The best scenario, of course, is for the OPP to seek counseling from a qualified therapist. If he or she won't, don't try to be helpful by suggesting that the OPP forgive the perpetrator. Only those who didn't mean harm or made mistakes and who ask forgiveness should be forgiven. Instead, urge your friend to release the bitterness because it's too heavy a burden to keep carrying. The past will always be what it was; it can't be changed. But by guiding the OPP to look ahead, without being dragged down by unhappy memories of the past, you can help your OPP enjoy the present with you and together you both can look toward a brighter future.

We encourage people who have been victimized to take revenge. And, of course, the best revenge is living well. It's a much more sane and effective approach to victimization. Dan, a twenty-year-old man who had been physically abused by his father, did seek counseling. Was he told that he had to forgive his father? No. Not, at least, until and unless his father begged or pleaded for forgiveness. But that didn't happen. In the meantime, the therapist suggested that Dan should take revenge. When he has children of his own, he should never hit them. Never. Loving his kids as he had wanted to be loved would be his revenge.

The worst thing that happens in so many cases is that the victim in some way identifies with the aggressor and becomes like him. Victims should focus on doing good and not assume that what happened to them was in any way their fault. If your friend was raped, try to encourage her to volunteer in a rape crisis center or to join a feminine group that focuses on this issue. If your friend is a male who has been traumatized, suggest he serve as a mentor to abused or neglected children. This would be the best revenge. By actively doing good works, the bitterness of the past could be dissipated. It doesn't help for someone to act as though his or her life is over based on past traumas. Try to motivate your OPP to change his or her thinking in some of the following ways:

- Remembering that no one should remain victimized by traumatic and agonizing experiences of the past
- Becoming hopeful about the possibilities of change
- Allowing positive revenge to help let go of feelings of unworthiness
- Focusing on being helpful to others

Psychologist Lauren Slater suggested in an article in the *New York Times* magazine section on February 23, 2003, that some traumatized people may be better off repressing the experience instead of illuminating it in therapy. For some people, rehashing the same incident makes them feel more anxiety. If this appears to be happening to your friend, consider encouraging him or her to terminate the treatment and make an effort to focus more on the present.

Author, explorer, and Nobel Peace Prize winner Fridtjof Nansen said: "I demolish my bridges behind me . . . then there is no choice but forward." So help your friend to demolish those unpleasant memories, to do good deeds for others, to learn something new, and to go into the current relationship with you with a smile.

What If Your OPP Is from a Different Religion or Ethnic Group?

This is a frequent problem. You're getting along great with your new computer date. You've finally met someone who's into folk dancing, bridge, and reading the old classics. You didn't think you'd ever meet such a person, and, in addition, he or she has a great personality, wonderful sense of humor, and is a terrific lover.

So what could be wrong? The problem is that your OPP is Catholic and you're Jewish. You've always maintained a Jewish home and celebrated Jewish holidays while your OPP goes to mass every Sunday and loves Christmas, especially the antique crèche and the Christmas tree with Mom's and Grandma's decorations on it. But your aging mother is upset that you're even dating a gentile, let alone considering marrying one. Fortunately, your adult kids aren't terribly concerned and, actually, one of them is also dating a gentile.

What bothers you? Is it that if this relationship continues and heads into a marriage you're worried about who will perform the wedding? Stop worrying about that, because many priests and rabbis officiate together at mixed marriages. Are you concerned about maintaining your traditions? Stop worrying about that as well. There's no reason you can't follow your own traditions and learn about those your OPP cherishes as well. Yours wouldn't be the first home to have both a menorah (at Chanukah) and a tree (at Christmas), with a mezuzah on the front door and a cross in the bedroom.

But what if one of you is very religious and gives priority to the religion over and above the relationship? Or, what happens if one partner doesn't want the other to maintain his or her religious traditions? That individual constantly—subtly and overtly—tries to convert you to his or her religion and beliefs. Then, to be very honest, the odds are good that there probably are going to be problems. Maybe you need to seek a relationship with someone who is more flexible.

The same is true if you develop a relationship with someone from a different ethnic background. Mixed-race marriages in the United States now number 1.5 million, with about 40 percent of Asian-Americans and 6 percent of blacks marrying whites. According to Randall Kennedy, author of *Interracial Intimacies*, "I do think it [interracial dating and marriage] is a good thing. It's a welcome sign of thoroughgoing desegregation. We talk about desegregation in the public sphere. Here's desegregation in the most intimate sphere."

It takes understanding to acknowledge that every culture has differences and to be accepting of them. Consider the example of a Christian Caucasian man who becomes involved in a relationship with a Hindu woman. He loves her strong sense of family, wit, and intelligence and has even become accustomed to the music that seems unusual to his ears and enjoys the varied vegetarian diet. But every so often, he really feels a need for a good piece of steak or a hamburger. Should he feel that he has to sneak it or can he talk about his need to maintain a little of his former diet? What about you, if you've been involved in a mixed-ethnic relationship? Have you ever asked your partner how he or she feels about the differences your culture presents? Finally, are your cultural differences really so great that you need to break off the growing and fond relationship?

What happens if you're black and find yourself attracted to a white person? Do you worry that your family members will be upset when they find out? Are you uncomfortable when you go out together, wondering what others may think? Perhaps it's time to give yourself a good talking to. Do you enjoy this person as a human being? Do you share some common interests and do you have fun together? Does he or she comfort you when you have personal or medical problems? Remember the words of Duc François de La Rochefoucauld, a French author and moralist, who said, "However rare true love may be, it is still less so than genuine friendship." There's nothing about the color of one's skin being a requirement for friendship or even a more personal relationship.

What If Your OPP Has a Disability or Chronic Illness?

Ellen's grandmother used to say, "Everyone has something. This is what you have." It wasn't a put-down; it was merely stating a reality. It's unlikely, at this stage of your life, that you'll find someone who doesn't have something—a slight deafness, arthritis, a mastectomy, asthma, a chronic disease such as diabetes or emphysema, and so on. But if you're waiting to find a good friend in later life who's a perfect physical specimen, you may have a long wait. Most of us have a little something, a little defect, a chronic ailment, or a major disability.

In my (Sol Gordon's) book *How Can You Tell If You're Really in Love?* I say: "False perceptions also color our view of people with disabilities. When we talk about potential partners, how many of us are open to the idea of meeting and falling in love with someone who is blind or in a wheelchair? If it's true that a person's values, personality, and character are important in a relationship, then why are many people uncomfortable when they first meet someone with a physical disability?"

Think about it. If a friend raves to you about a person he or she wants you to meet, saying, "You two would be perfect for each other," does your enthusiasm suddenly waver when your friend adds, "He needs a wheelchair"? If you do hesitate in agreeing to meet this almost perfect person, then slow down and think about it. That individual might be great fun to be with, a terrific cook, extremely popular, caring, and just the person you've been looking for as a special friend and, perhaps, a more serious relationship. Why miss the opportunity to meet someone that outstanding just because he needs a wheelchair to get around? Consider your actions if you had met and committed to this person when he was still able to walk and then an accident occurred and he needed a wheelchair. Would you feel different about him now that he's disabled? Probably not, so why build walls to separate you from possibilities today?

The same message is true for someone who has had a mastectomy, is blind, or may have one of a number of different disabilities or chronic illnesses such as Crohn's disease, diabetes, Parkinson's disease, or chronic obstructive pulmonary disease (emphysema and chronic bronchitis). You may feel a little shy, at first, not knowing what to say or how to behave. The best way is to ask how the other person wants to be treated. For example, "Do you want me to take your arm when we cross the street?" gives an option to someone who is blind. He or she can either accept your offer or say no and tell you why. Some people with disabilities and chronic illnesses don't mind talking about their problems while others tend to be a little introspective, but most individuals don't want to be considered "different" or "fragile."

Treat a person with disabilities as you would anyone else you meet. Don't become overprotective and do everything for the other person. No one wants to feel helpless. Take your cue from that individual.

If your friendship progresses into a more intimate relationship, learn as much as you can about your partner's disability or illness, especially when it comes to sexual issues. Understand the effects, not only of the disease, but also of the medications used to treat the disease. Speak openly and honestly about ways to be physically intimate without causing pain or discomfort.

If you are the person with a disability, try to filter out any images you may have of what the perfect person looks like and stop comparing yourself with some idea of perfection. Focus instead on positive thoughts of yourself as a special human being with unique gifts and much to offer in a friendship. Here are some suggestions for you:

- Visualize yourself mixing with other people and open yourself to the friendship of others. If you don't see yourself as "defective," others won't either.
- Develop your interests, and people will be interested in you.
- Find confidence in yourself and your giving, caring nature, and realize that everyone has some type of problem; this will endear you to others.
- Focus on friendships first, as we've said many times. Personal, close relationships grow from the seeds of friendships.

Friendship should be blind when it comes to disabilities. Show others than you're a person first and that your disability or chronic illness is secondary to everything else that is important about you. You are not your disability. We like the quote from former first lady Abigail Adams, who said, "It is not in the still calm of life, or the repose of a pacific station, that great characters are formed . . . Great necessities call out great virtues."

Choosing to Leave or Stay

A great deal of our advice has dealt with ways to take a second look at the OPP to determine whether the sticky point is something that you could overlook or learn to live with in order to continue a relationship, or if it is a "deal breaker," even if this person is otherwise a perfect person for you. Think twice when the otherwise perfect person . . .

- Doesn't listen to you. You never hear phrases such as "I see what you mean," or "I understand," "I think you handled it well," or even "Un huh." The person may read the paper or actually get up and walk out of a room as you're talking.
- Is self-absorbed and thinks only in terms of how things pertain to or affect him or her.
- Breaks promises and gives lame excuses why.
- Cries often and is depressed most of the time.
- Lies or exaggerates a lot.
- Blames you when things go wrong in his or her life.
- Is preoccupied with his or her own needs.
- Always wants to be the center of attention.
- Is jealous of your friends and resents your family, especially if you're particularly close to them.
- Is disrespectful to you and to your friends and family.
- Stirs up feelings of insecurity in you.
- Seems too needy with comments of dependency that

masquerade as love, such as "I can't live without you" and "Without you my life is meaningless."

• Isn't willing to talk about issues you consider important.

On the other hand, when the relationship has a healthy focus, the chances for success are greatly improved. Psychoanalyst and author Erich Fromm put it just right when he wrote in *The Art of Loving*: If there is a potential for intimacy, this is what happens:

• "There is caring deeply about your partner's welfare and growth.
• There is respecting your partner's identity—for their right to be who they are, rather than how you would like them to be.
• There is taking responsibility to care for the other person in an involved, active way.
• There is acknowledging the other person—his or her values, needs, desires, dreams, foibles."

Everyone has faults, and you need to think about your values and what you want in a person with whom you are sharing a great deal of your life. Don't settle for a relationship that doesn't feel right to you. As Judy (not her real name) said, "I go with my gut feeling. Do I have a good time? Do I feel relaxed? Did he say anything that makes me uncomfortable? Do I feel like it's okay to just be myself with him?"

Unfortunately, there's no test or rules. In the end, it has to be what seems right to you. Good luck.

Chapter 10

Sharpening Communication Skills

"Listening, not imitation, may be the sincerest form of flattery."

—Dr. Joyce Brothers, psychologist and television personality

MOST OF US PROBABLY define "communication" as the act of speaking. But just having the ability to form recognizable words has as little to do with real communication as the ability to walk has to do with running a marathon. It's a beginning, nothing more. Without effective communication, any relationship is functioning with a serious handicap. It's like operating a delicate piece of machinery without the instruction manual. You may get it working, but you won't know what button to push when it gets out of kilter.

While you may have been communicating just fine with your family and friends, you may suddenly find yourself a little tongue-tied and self-conscious when it comes to meeting new people, especially those you'd like to see more of and perhaps develop an intimate relationship with. True communication is a process involving interaction between the speaker and the listener; we can give you a few pointers that may help you sharpen your communication skills.

It Takes Two to Communicate

When you're the listener, you have the responsibility to do the
following:

• *Pay attention to the speaker and don't let your mind
wander.* To determine if you're guilty of letting your mind
wander when someone is speaking, think back to the last time
you drove into a gas station to ask for directions. The atten-
dant talked, pointed, and you nodded as though you understood. Then you said "thanks," and drove off, not having a
clue what you just heard. That's called "idle listening." While it
can cause you to get lost when you're driving in the car, it can
also drive away a potential relationship when you're beginning to date.

• *Maintain eye contact, unless it isn't accepted in your culture.* Many Native Americans and Asian-Americans avoid eye
contact to show respect, while some Hispanics feel that certain
people possess the "evil eye" and that, by staring at another individual, they can cause harm to that person. Otherwise, be sure
to look at the person you're talking to.

• *Give proper feedback, either verbally or nonverbally, to let
the speaker know the message is being received.* Feedback may be
as little as occasionally saying, "I see," or by nodding your head,
or paraphrasing what you've heard by saying, "Do you mean
you really don't want to go?" or "I don't understand why you're
angry. Could you explain?" Don't be surprised if what you
hear isn't always what the speaker meant. That's called
"crossover" speech, and it frequently is the cause of arguments
and misunderstandings.

• *Refrain from using body language that shows you're disinterested, bored, or in a hurry to get away.* That includes fidgeting,
looking at your watch, glancing at the newspaper, or tapping

your fingers. It's important to remember that more than half of what we communicate is expressed in body language, including changes in postures, hand gestures, and facial expressions. According to Florence Wolff, professor emeritus of the University of Dayton and an expert on listening skills, "There are two hundred thirty-five different facial expressions." You may think you're listening intently, but your body language sends a different message, one that can be readily understood by the other person.

• *Listen without interrupting or thinking about what you're going to say next.* "I am convinced," said Rabbi Richard Birnholz of Congregation Schaarai Zedek in Tampa, Florida, "that most miscommunication occurs because instead of listening, instead of really listening, we are too busy holding hearings. And there is a difference between listening and holding a hearing. When we listen, we put the other person first. We respond to *their* needs and react sensitively to their feelings. When we hold hearings, we put ourselves first and listen judgmentally. We begin with our own agenda and then, without listening to the other person at all, make our point or make the other person's word fit our expectations."

When you're the speaker, you have the responsibility to do the following:

• *Watch nonverbal clues and ask questions.* Be sure the listener is hearing the message you're giving.
• *Don't monopolize the conversation.* Pause to give the other person a chance to speak as well. In a true conversation, there should be a gentle give and take. If you find your listener becoming glassy-eyed, it may be that you're delivering a monologue rather than taking part in a conversation.

Does this sound like a lot of work? Not if you want to really communicate effectively.

Listen to What's Not Being Said

There's more to a message than what's actually being said. Your communication with someone new on a first or second date can give you a great deal of information if you listen carefully and read between the lines. For example, you can quickly tell if the other person is negative or depressed. Consider this actual conversation:

> *You:* "It's a beautiful day today, isn't it?"
> *New friend:* "It'll rain."
> *You:* "Well, maybe so, but we need the rain. It's been such a dry summer."
> *New friend:* "Everything's dead. I lost all my plants!"
> *You:* "Would it help if you watered them?"
> *New friend:* [shrug] "What's the use?"
> *You:* [hopefully] "It might revive them."
> *New friend:* "I don't like them anyway."

It doesn't sound as though this would be a friend you'd enjoy getting to know any better because this person sounds negative, possibly depressed, and certainly is no fun to talk to. But perhaps you also need to consider the messages *you're* sending as well. Do you talk about your lousy relationship with your kids? Your most recent operation or illness? Why the world's going to hell under the present administration? Might you be talking yourself out of a potential relationship?

Try to be positive in your messages when you meet new people, remembering that a pleasant expression also makes you more interesting to listen to. While you don't want to be considered a Pollyanna, think about the way a conversation's going and try to keep it upbeat.

Learn the Communication Dialect

Just as different areas of the United States speak the English language with unique dialects, individuals do, too. We all speak differently depending on the circumstances and to whom we're speaking. Most of us have separate business, social, and personal modes of communication.

In a business situation, our vocabulary may be more formal, we may keep our bodies more erect, our voices may have less expression, while in personal relationships we tend to use more slang, our bodies may be more relaxed and less inhibited, and our faces may show subtle nuances of tenderness, sexuality, or affection. The difficulty often arises when there is spillover from our business communication into our personal life causing someone you have just met to find you unfriendly or unapproachable. To prevent this from happening, give yourself a breather between coming from work and meeting new social contacts.

Another way to avoid communication spillover is to become more aware of how you're feeling in a particular situation and to stay aware of your listener's reactions. While you may be enthusiastic about your line of work and want to tell others about it, you need to remember that most jobs have their own terminology or dialects that others don't understand. If you don't explain the terms, others will be confused.

A good example of communication spillover is the word "sidebar." It has different meanings for a lawyer (to approach the bench and communicate with the judge), a decorator (a piece of furniture, usually in the dining room), and a writer (extra information that doesn't fit within the body of an article so it's boxed in on the side of the page). Same word; different meanings.

Because we all were raised in different families, we've grown up with unique communication styles that may be misunderstood by a newcomer. You may feel comfortable in a home where a lot of joking, sarcasm, and yelling is common, whereas the person you're dating is used to soft tones, slow speech, and thoughtful discussion. Some of us were raised in households where certain subjects (sex, finance, illness, or death) were never mentioned and are bewildered and often bothered when we date someone who is used to discussing openly and honestly these and other subjects that we think of as taboo.

It takes time to recognize and become accustomed to communication differences and to not feel threatened by them. It helps if you give immediate feedback, such as, "I'm not used to talking about death and dying. It seems strange and a little uncomfortable to me right now. Can we talk about something else?" or "Why are you being sarcastic with me? Are you angry?"

Asking these types of questions gives the other person notice that you aren't speaking the same dialect so he or she can modify his or her language to make you more comfortable and prevent problems or misunderstandings. Don't expect the other person to read your mind and don't try to read his or hers. Most of us aren't blessed with mind-reading skills. Relationships can't grow when the foundation's paved with guesswork.

What's important is that communication works for you both and that one person isn't taking advantage of the other. No two people will balance exactly even on the teeter-totter of a relationship all of the time, but it's important that one person isn't always flying high while the other is sitting on the ground, wondering when it's his or her turn to be up in the air.

Show Respect and Trust

Developing strong communication skills between you and another as you begin to date and form a more lasting relationship is important in order to maintain balance. That's where trust and respect come in. If he says he doesn't mind if you go out for dinner with your women friends or she says it's okay for you to go to the ball game with the guys, and then there's silence or pouting the next time you're together, it belies the honesty you thought was present in the communication exchange. If you get the third degree when you're not home when he calls, and he doesn't accept your honest excuse that you were tied up in traffic or waiting for a prescription to be filled at the drugstore, you need to talk about the importance of trust and respect.

Does Your Relationship Need a Communication Makeover?

You may have been going along in a relationship, thinking everything was just fine, only to have your bubble burst when your partner says, "This isn't working. We never talk anymore." Your first thought is "That's crazy. We talk all the time." You may be talking, all right, but the truth is, you may not be communicating. The meaning of this powerful complaint goes much deeper than the two of you not talking to each other. It is an indication that one or more of these problems exist:

- Your partner doesn't think you listen (and perhaps you don't).
- You don't talk about anything that is important to your partner. Listen to what you're saying. Is it gossip? Household

chatter? What happened on the latest soap or retelling the play-by-play of a football game?

- You don't talk on an honest level with one another.
- The two of you use television as a buffer to meaningful conversation.
- You both try to have others around—double-dating, traveling, or having dinner with another couple—so you can't have meaningful conversation.
- You seldom confide in one another because one or both of you have used that information in the past as a weapon against the other in an argument or have betrayed the confidence by repeating it to others.
- Neither of you is willing to talk about problems in your relationship for fear of saying something in anger that you'll regret.

Issues such as these can affect the quality of your relationship and prevent true intimacy and closeness from developing. Fortunately, however, you can learn to improve your conversation skills so you feel comfortable expressing yourself and know that your partner has received an accurate translation of your message.

How to Improve Your Communication Skills

How can you improve your communication skills so you can determine whether you just aren't communicating well or if the relationship isn't a healthy one and maybe you should call it quits? Here are some suggestions:

- *Make your meaning clear.* Don't use kidding or sarcasm to mask your meaning. It only confuses the issue. If it's something that's important to you, think about it before you put it into words. Make notes if you need to at first.

- *Ask for feedback.* Remember the children's game of "Telephone" where someone whispered into the next person's ear and that person repeated what he or she thought the message was until it went full circle, sometimes with hilarious results? The confusion and misinformation might have been good fun then, but it can play havoc in adult life. Don't be hesitant to ask the other person to repeat what he or she thought you said. Don't be surprised if it isn't what you meant.

- *Give your full attention to your partner.* That means putting down the newspaper or book, turning off the radio or television, laying your knitting or needlepoint down, and focusing on what's being said and how it's being said.

- *Give active feedback.* Nod your head, say "okay," "I see," or "un huh." Some experts suggest paraphrasing what the other person has said, giving him or her the opportunity to say "Right, that's just what I meant," or "No, that's not what I meant at all." That offers the chance for the individual to rephrase in order to get the message across.

- *Make "I" statements.* Stay away from statements that begin "You always . . ." or "You never . . ." That creates a situation where the other person will go on the defensive. Better to say "I feel lonely when you're gone all day Saturday playing golf with the guys" or "I feel very stressed out with so much clutter around. What can we do to minimize the piles of stuff?"

- *Share feelings as well as thoughts.* Remember when you were a child and came home to report that you were afraid of the school bully or that you thought the teacher hated you? Your parents said, "That's silly," and by doing so, dismissed your feelings as unimportant. But whether or not we agree with another's feelings, we should, at least, acknowledge them. When we recognize another's feelings, we acknowledge them, giving them form and substance. Instead of floating around like vapor, these feelings become visible and can be dealt with. When people become blocked by their feelings, thought processes also can become inhibited.

- *Get help if you need it.* Put some money where your heart is and consider signing up for a relationship or communication course given by a therapist, member of the clergy, or a communication educator at your local university or community college. These courses are often given over the weekend or one night a week for a set period at a conference center, college classroom, or a religious or retreat facility. Be sure it's a course that isn't for married couples only, and be sure it includes communication in relationships. Also, be sure to ask for the names of some older unmarried individuals who have taken the course so you can ask them if they recommend it as a valuable resource.

We All Need a Communication Tuneup

You may believe taking a communication course is silly, a waste of time, and is only for young kids who don't know their own minds. But the truth is that many older people need help with their communication skills. Perhaps faulty communication is one of the root causes of a previous relationship not working out.

The verbal shorthand you may have used with a previous partner may not be as effective with your new partner. (And it may not have been effective with your old one, either.) Some people who live together for many years can almost read each other's mind, saying something the other is just about to say. But, without realizing it, you may be expecting or assuming that the new person in your life can do the same thing. This will result only in frustration for you and bewilderment for your new partner.

Learning how to communicate honestly and effectively with your new special friend will be exhilarating. It can improve your self-esteem because you know that the one you care for completely understands what you're saying and that you can be honest about how you're feeling on any issue. You can share your values and your thoughts without worrying about misunderstandings. If confusion should arise, the two of you can calmly discuss the problem without anger, ridicule, or sarcasm.

You remember what you told your kids when they were little and whiney: "Use your words rather than whining so I can understand what you want." Now that you both are speaking the "same" language, you can freely do just that. There's no code, no games, no subtle subtext, just open communication, which frees you and draws you closer to your potential partner.

Chapter 11

Sex Isn't a
Four-Letter Word

"Sex has become one of the most discussed subjects of modern times. The Victorians pretended it did not exist; the moderns pretend that nothing else exists."

—Fulton John Sheen (1895–1979),
American Roman Catholic bishop

Contrary to what most young people think, older folks "do it," too. You're never too old to enjoy physical intimacy, be it cuddling, mutual masturbation, or sexual intercourse. Sex can be fun, delightful, satisfying, and sensual. It helps if men pop the question: "What is it that you most enjoy?" and that women answer truthfully. According to authors Paula Brown Doress-Worters and Diana Laskin Siegal, in their book *Ourselves Growing Older*, "research demonstrates that clitoral, vaginal, and uterine stimulation or a combination of these leads to orgasm" and it need not necessarily be the result of penile penetration.

As you reclaim physical intimacy, be sure you set the scene that makes it conducive for both of you. You'll know when you're ready. The stereotype ideas of candlelit dinners, strolls in the moonlight, a warm bath for two, and even skinny dipping can become erotic turn-ons for you. Remember the scene in the movie *From Here to Eternity* when Burt Lancaster made love to

Deborah Kerr on the beach as the waves lapped over them? Those are images you need to remember.

Find the time of day that works best for you. You both may be too tired in the evening and "dopey" in the morning. If so, remember the joys of the "matinee." Put the telephone answering machine on, lock the door if you have children (now adults themselves, who think nothing of still coming inside your home without announcing their presence), and enjoy yourselves. If the first time isn't completely satisfactory, don't get discouraged. It often takes awhile for people to become sexually compatible. Remember to keep your sense of humor, too. Lovemaking should be fun.

You may have thought of your sexual life in the past tense. After all, you have no special person in your life anymore and you can't imagine having a new sexual partner at this stage of your life. You're too old, too wrinkled, too flabby, too out of practice, too whatever. But it's time for a change of attitude. According to a study by the National Council on the Aging (NCOA) . . .

- 71 percent of men and 51 percent of women in their sixties are sexually active.
- 57 percent of men and 30 percent of women in their seventies are sexually active.
- When asked about the emotional satisfaction they received from their sex lives, 74 percent of the sexually active men and 70 percent of the sexually active women said they are as satisfied or even more satisfied than they were in their forties, probably because there were no young children around to interrupt, the demands of an outside job may be lessened, and they were generally more relaxed.
- Nearly half of all Americans age sixty or older engage in

sexual activity at least once a month and four in ten want to have sex more frequently than they currently do.

"Our study," said James Firman, president and CEO of NCOA, "debunks the prevailing myths about sexuality in older years. For many older Americans, sex remains an important and vital part of their lives."

Studies have shown that even without partners, older people often practice self-arousal (masturbation). In her book *I'm Too Young to Get Old*, Dr. Judith Reichman wrote that "self-arousal will bring sexual pleasure and should not be thought of with shame or embarrassment." She continues: "Several recent studies have shown that more than 70 percent of American women masturbate and that 37 percent of women in their sixties continue (or begin) to do so. Masturbation, just like intercourse, will help us maintain our vulvar and vaginal health after menopause."

How to Rekindle Sexuality Again

It's natural to be a little anxious when you think about resuming sexual intimacy, especially if you've been abstinent for a time. You may have considered that aspect of your life to be over and stopped thinking of yourself as a desirable and sexual human being. Both men and women may feel it is "unseemly" to think of sex in later life. Men may worry about an inability to "perform" with a new person. But, according to the NCOA, finding sexual fulfillment later in life is not only a realistic goal, but it's a very healthy and positive one. If sex hasn't been in the picture for some time, it's very understandable to feel nervous about starting to date again and wondering how to handle the physical side of intimacy if and when it arises.

You might begin to prepare for the dating scene by making an appointment with a physician to discuss sexual issues such as lack of desire, inhibition, lack of lubrication causing vaginal discomfort, erectile dysfunction, and other problems that concern you. You may feel embarrassed to think of discussing this delicate and most personal issue with a stranger, but most physicians are used to hearing these common problems and can help you. If you feel uncomfortable with your present doctor, ask for a referral to a geriatrician (if your community has such a specialist), a urologist, a sex therapist, or a gynecologist. You may prefer a doctor your own age or gender, or possibly someone younger who you perceive to be more comfortable talking about sexual issues. Be sure to mention the medications you're presently taking because many of them can contribute to sexual dysfunction.

You should also be sure to discuss safe sex with your doctor. While pregnancy may no longer be a concern, sexually transmitted diseases are an increasing problem in older Americans.

What You Need to Know About Sexually Transmitted Diseases

Unless you decide that you're going to be celibate—and that's okay if that's your preference—there is no 100 percent guaranteed way to avoid being exposed to sexually transmitted diseases (STDs) if you're sexually active. Even if you or your partner is postmenopausal, the need for condoms is just as strong—remember, it's not just about birth control, it's about preventing the spread of sexually transmitted disease. You can practice safe sex by using latex condoms with every act of sexual intercourse until you're in a monogamous relationship for at least six months or more. After that time, both you and your partner should be tested for STDs, and, we hope, both of you are found negative. Be aware, however, that someone can be infected with the HIV virus for several years before it shows up on a test. Sally, a woman from Colorado in her late fifties who was married twice (divorced once and widowed once), offers this advice on sexual matters: "Trust no one, be very careful, and be prepared. Don't even think of not using a condom."

Although sex can make you feel alive and young again, it also has a dark side. In a 2001 report, former Surgeon General David Satcher listed promoting responsible sexual behaviors as one of the surgeon general's public health priorities. Responsible sexual behavior is also one of the ten leading health indicators according to Healthy People 2010, the federal government's blueprint for building a healthier nation over the next ten years. While it's important to acknowledge the many positive benefits of sexuality (such as women maintaining the strength of their pubococcygeus muscle, which is involved in preventing urinary stress incontinence, creating a sense of well-being and joy, and fulfilling the need to be touched), we also need to understand that there are undesirable consequences as well—alarming high levels of sexually transmitted disease, including HIV/AIDS infection, and unintended pregnancy, abortion, sexual dysfunction, and sexual violence.

In the United States . . .

- STDs infect approximately 12 million persons each year.
- 775,000 AIDS cases have been reported since 1981, and nearly two-thirds were sexually transmitted.
- An estimated 800,000 to 900,000 persons are living with HIV.
- An estimated one-third of those living with HIV are aware of their status and are in treatment; one-third are aware, but not in treatment; and one-third have not been tested and are not aware.

- An estimated 40,000 new HIV infections occur each year.
- An estimated 22 percent of women and 2 percent of men have been victims of a forced sexual act.

A public health problem exists. Five of the ten most commonly reported infectious diseases in the United States, 87 percent of the cases according to a 1997 report by the Institute of Medicine, are STDs. These diseases are becoming prevalent in postmenopausal women who, because they no longer worry about pregnancy, don't require their sexual partners to use protection. Nevertheless, public awareness regarding STDs is not widespread, nor is their disproportionate impact on women, adolescents, and racial and ethnic minorities well known. Consider these facts:

- Chlamydia infection is the most commonly reported STD. While reported rates of infection in women greatly exceed those in men (largely because screening programs have been primarily directed toward women), the rates for both women and men are probably similar.
- It is estimated that 45 million persons in the United States are infected with genital herpes and one million new cases occur each year.
- Human papillomavirus (HPV) is a sexually transmitted virus that causes genital warts. An estimated 5.5 million persons become infected with HPV each year in this country, and an estimated 20 million are currently infected. There are many different types of HPV. While most women who have HPV do not develop cervical cancer, four HPV subtypes are responsible for an estimated 80 percent of cervical cancer cases, with approximately 14,000 new cervical cancer cases occurring per year.

- Since 1981, a total of more than 775,000 AIDS cases have been reported to the Center for Disease Control (CDC). The disease has disproportionately affected men who have sex with men—47 percent of reported AIDS cases. Of this number, minority men have now emerged as the population most affected. A recently released seven-city survey indicates that new HIV infection is substantially higher for young Black gay and bisexual men than for their White or Hispanic counterparts. During the 1990s, the epidemic also shifted toward women. While women account for 28 percent of the HIV cases reported since 1981, they account for 32 percent of those reported between July 1999 and June 2000. Similarly, women account for 17 percent of AIDS cases reported since 1981, but 24 percent of those reported between July 1999 and June 2000.

Myths and Facts About STDs

It's important to know what's true and what's hearsay when it comes to STDs. Michael Shapiro, R.N., C.F.N.P., M.S.N., in the clinical journal *Nursing2000* (May, 2000), describes several commonly held misunderstandings about what screening tests work for diagnosing STDs, what treatments are available, and more:

Myth: Condom use prevents the spread of all sexually transmitted diseases.
Fact: Although condom use will help prevent STDs such as gonorrhea, syphilis, and chlamydia, other STDs such as herpes simplex virus (HSV) and human papillomavirus (HPV) can be transmitted in spite of appropriate condom use.

Myth: Treating STDs usually involves complex drug regimens administered over several weeks.

Fact: A one-time, single-dose treatment effectively eradicates many uncomplicated infections, including gonorrhea, chlamydia, trichomoniasis, syphilis, bacterial vaginosis, vulvovaginal candidiasis, scabies, and pediculosis pubis (lice) infestation. Complicated cases may require a more complicated dosing schedule.

Myth: All STDs can be cured.

Fact: Although many STDs are curable, no cure is available for hepatitis, HPV, HSV, and HIV infections. However, treatments are available to manage these infections. Several oral and topical antiviral medications are available to reduce the severity of HSV outbreaks. Podophyllum resin, interferon inducers, electrocautery, cryotherapy, laser therapy, and liquid nitrogen are used to treat HPV infections with varying degrees of success.

Myth: Most STDs produce clinical signs and symptoms that aid diagnosis.

Fact: Because almost all STDs can be asymptomatic or have subclinical symptoms, diagnosing the disease by clinical signs and symptoms alone may be impossible. Lab tests such as serology or cultures of drainage from the urethra or vagina will confirm the diagnosis of an STD.

Myth: A Papanicolaou test (Pap smear) is a good screening test for STDs.

Fact: A Pap smear can help identify cellular changes caused by current infection with HPV, HSV, and trichomoniasis. But it's not a good screening test for the actual presence of STDs and should never be substituted for other STD screening tests. Serologic tests or body-fluid cultures are two reliable tests used for STD screening.

If you become sexually active with a new partner, be sure to practice safe sex by using a latex condom every time you have vaginal, anal, or oral sex. Avoid contact with body fluids and have regular checkups.

Sex Is Only One Aspect of a Relationship

There are four important messages relating to sex. Each one is important to remember:

1. You can have what you think is great sex and still have a lousy relationship.
2. You can have great sex and it can greatly enhance your relationship. Don't forget this critical message: It is always important for a man or woman to ask the other what he or she likes—what turns the individual on. People are often surprised at the response they get.
3. You can't judge a relationship by what happens during the initial experiments with sex. People can be dysfunctionally orgasmic and still care a lot about each other.
4. Be honest, open, and nonjudgmental.

It's extremely important to be honest with a potential sexual partner if you've had or are having any type of sexual dysfunction. Otherwise, he or she may feel you're not interested or develop doubts concerning an ability to satisfy you. This can negatively affect a blooming relationship before you have the chance to determine if the dysfunction can be treated or how important it is to your developing relationship. Often, it's not a "deal breaker."

Also, be honest if you don't feel you're ready for sexual intimacy. If the other person respects and cares for you, he or she will understand and work with you to find other ways to cuddle and show affection. Don't ever let yourself be talked into having sexual intercourse if you don't want to. Follow your instincts. If it means losing the attention of someone you hoped might become special to you, perhaps it's good that you found out early in the relationship.

Dealing with Lack of Desire

So often, lack of desire has to do with lack of opportunity with the right person, although it also can be due to other factors, such as medication, alcohol and/or drug abuse, or other health problems. Many postmenopausal women, for instance, suffer from a lack of sexual desire or an ability to become physically aroused. It can be caused by a variety of problems, such as lack of natural vaginal lubrication, inhibition, hormonal changes, or anxiety, as well as inflammation of the vagina that can be a result of sexually transmitted diseases.

Men, on the other hand, may suffer from impotence, also known (thanks to advertising by Senator Dole) as erectile dysfunction. Research from the Massachusetts Male Aging Study revealed that 34.8 percent of men ages forty to seventy had moderate to complete erectile dysfunction. The National Institutes of Health Consensus Panel described erectile dysfunction as an important public health problem despite the fact that sexual dysfunction is more prevalent for women (43 percent) than for men (31 percent). Men also may suffer from premature ejaculation and/or low desire for sex.

What to Do When Your Sex Drive Goes

As mentioned before, there are all kinds of reasons why "sex" doesn't work for you—disease, alcohol abuse, the effect of medications, and psychological issues. Sex therapy and Viagra don't always work, and ignoring or avoiding the issue certainly doesn't help, either.

An article by Karen S. Peterson in *USA TODAY* (January 23, 2003) suggests that there are 40 million Americans who are "mired in low-sex or no-sex marriages." There are also many single Americans who wonder why their sex drive or ability has abandoned them. Large numbers of men of all ages rarely desire their wives or significant others sexually or rarely have sexual partners because of a variety of physical and emotional factors.

An important article appearing in the "Health and Fitness" section of the *New York Times* regarding efforts to create a Viagra equivalent for women observed that desire blends with arousal in both men and women. But desire may be lacking in each sex because of our increasingly busy lives trying to juggle work, exercise, child or aging-parent care, home responsibilities, and so on. According to the book *The Sex-Starved Marriage* by therapist Michele Weiner-Davis, millions of American marriages involve little or no sex often because husbands are not interested. Barry and Emily McCarthy estimate in their book *Rekindling Desire: A Step-by-Step Program to Help Low-Sex and No-Sex Marriages* that about one adult man in six and one adult woman in three have little or no interest in sex at all.

This may be so, but this should not be a good enough reason to avoid the lack of intimacy. There is always cuddling, hugging, mutual massage, bathing or showering together, and mutual masturbation. If couples are just "too tired" for even those physical forms of affection, perhaps they should get a physical checkup by their physician and, if all checks out all right, should turn off the late news and go to bed earlier. Here are some suggestions to encourage physical intimacy:

- Speak honestly about your sexual likes and dislikes.
- Share your sexual fantasies.
- Listen to and respect your partner's taboos.
- Take a vacation—even to a local hotel—if you feel inhibited at home.
- Take turns massaging each other to learn what touches are preferred.
- Be forgiving when an intimate session turns out less than perfect.
- Keep your sense of humor.
- Focus on the feelings of your lovemaking, not the appearance or lack of an orgasm.
- Accept your physical appearance and that of your partner.
- Keep communication lines open.
- Accept yourself.

When Medication Affects Sexual Function

One seldom-discussed cause of sexual dysfunction when you get older is that after age sixty, most adults are taking a variety of medications—often eight or more—some of which either lower libido or cause sexual dysfunction. Both men and women can experience these side effects from drugs as common as antidepressants, some ulcer medications, and heart and blood pressure medications. Even well-known antihistamines, such as Benadryl, can affect your sex life because, well, they dry up everything.

But you shouldn't stop taking these drugs even if you believe they're affecting your sex life. Instead, talk honestly with your physician to see if there is a substitute medication you might take that would have fewer side effects and still have a positive affect on your health. If your doctor doesn't seem too knowledgeable about potential side effects or minimizes the problem these side effects cause you, seek a second opinion. You also can get a copy of the *Physicians' Desk Reference* (PDR) at your library or local bookstore and look up side effects of various medications. Another good reference book to help you check out potential side effects is *The American Druggist's Complete Family Guide to Prescriptions, Pills, and Drugs.*

Sex therapists suggest that if you suddenly find that you're experiencing sexual dysfunction or loss of libido and have just begun to take a new medication, you should consider the medication to be the culprit until it's proven innocent. And, in the future, if the doctor prescribes a new medication, ask if it has any side effects that may affect you sexually.

Are You in a Low-Sex or No-Sex Relationship?

To determine if your relationship is low or no sex, take this test from *Rekindling Desire: A Step-by-Step Program to Help Low-Sex and No-Sex Marriages*, coauthored by Barry and Emily McCarthy. Answer true or false to the following statements:

- Sex is more work than play.
- Touching always leads to intercourse.
- Touching takes place only in the bedroom.
- You no longer look forward to making love.
- Sex does not give you feelings of connection or sharing.
- You never have sexual thoughts or fantasies about your partner.
- Sex is limited to a fixed time, such as Saturday night.

- One of you is the initiator, and the other feels pressured.
- You look back on premarital sex as the best sex.
- Sex has become routine.
- You have sex about once or twice a month or less.

Scoring: If you answered true to five or more statements, or true to the last one, you are in a low-sex or possibly a no-sex relationship.

If you feel troubled about sexual issues, talk to each other before you do anything else. Describe what turns you off as well as what turns you on. Are your breasts sensitive, so you don't like them being squeezed or even touched? Does breathing in your ear bother you rather than excite you? Are you ticklish in certain areas? If so, speak up. Experiment with mutual massage (without intercourse) to see what feels good to each of you, and speak up. Don't keep it a secret. You can also try mutual masturbation and give each other feedback as to what feels good and what doesn't.

But if one or both of you don't find mutual pleasure in having sex, and if this is perceived by either of you as a meaningful aspect of your life, consider sex therapy with a qualified counselor. You can get a list of qualified sex therapists in your area by contacting the American Association of Sex Therapists, P.O. Box 5488, Richmond, VA 23220-0488, or by logging on to *http://aasect@aasect.org*. We also recommend a very important book called *Beyond Orgasm—Dare to Be Honest about the Sex You Really Want* by Marty Klein. Shere Hite, author of *The Hite Report*, recommended this book by saying it's "the best resource available for thinking for yourself about sex." For people over sixty, we recommend *The New Love and Sex After 60* by Robert N. Butler and Myra I. Lewis and *Still Doing It: Women and Men Over 60 Write about Their Sexuality*, edited by Joani Blank.

But—and this is important—if sex is not really that crucial for either of you, it's okay.

What If Sex Isn't That Crucial for Either of You?

You may find as you get to know someone that although you enjoy his or her company tremendously and receive pleasure from dancing, hand-holding, and other similar nonsexual touches, that you really don't want to move on to a sexual relationship. There's nothing wrong with that, providing you're honest with the other person.

Never lead your partner on, pretending that "soon" you'll be ready. Instead, initiate open communication. You really don't need an excuse, so don't say, "I feel it would be disloyal to my dear dead wife," or "I'm too self-conscious about my scars [weight, and so on]." Just explain that you really don't want a sexual relationship, although you really enjoy the other's companionship. You may find that your partner's in total agreement and you can continue with a close emotional, but nonsexual relationship. Your partner really has three choices in response. He or she can (1) say "That's not what I want," and call it quits; (2) agree to those terms; or (3) agree to your terms "for now" and hope to persuade you differently. Who knows? As time goes on, you, too, may change your mind.

However, if you do desire sexual relations and you're starting out afresh in a new relationship, be careful. Every single sexually transmitted disease that we know about is on the increase from last year. Protect yourself. If a man says to you, "I get no feeling when I use a condom," your response should be "That's strange. All the other men I've slept with got plenty of feeling using a condom. What's the matter with you?"

Fantasies Are Normal

For some, the visual stimulation of pornography is particularly erotic and related to primitive pleasure centers. For others, specific scents or sounds are erotic. These various stimulations actually enhance our imagination, our capacity to fantasize, and to pleasure ourselves and each other. It's important to understand that erotic dreams, thoughts, and fantasies are normal. We all have them, and they arise from the unconscious mind over which we have very little control. They even occur while we're asleep. There's no sense wasting energy feeling guilty about thoughts or urges that pop into our minds.

In fact, if you feel guilty about a thought or fantasy, you'll have that thought over and over again, because guilt is the energy for its repetition. Once you realize that, you can enjoy your fantasies or let them go. If you find them disturbing, you can also dismiss them. Once you accept that everyone has them, that they're normal, you can choose to indulge them as long as they don't hurt or humiliate anyone else or let them go. No harm done. The mind is just doing what it does. Behavior can be abnormal or destructive, but not thoughts themselves unless you allow them to monopolize your life.

Can We Trust Sex Surveys?

Not entirely. So don't beat yourself up if a survey "reveals" that most people your age are having sex every night (and twice on Saturday) and experience an orgasm 99.9 percent of the time. It's not necessarily true, despite what you've read in a newspaper or magazine. In an article reviewing two biographies of Alfred Kinsey, Sarah Boxer (*The New York Times,* July 22, 2000) suggested that "people lie about sex. Those who don't lie often say inaccurate things. And most sex researchers aren't exactly neutral."

So why do we even read sex surveys? Because it's normal to want to know how we compare to everyone else, even though we don't know who these other people are as individuals or what their lives may be like. But the truth is, it really doesn't matter what others are doing, only what feels good and right to us. Sex is not an Olympic event on which we are judged. It's an immensely personal act that we share with someone we feel close and safe with, someone with whom we want to have a continued relationship (at least for awhile).

So forget about performance. It doesn't matter how long an erection lasted, whether there were simultaneous orgasms, or even how long the foreplay lasted. It isn't even significant if there was actual intercourse. What matters is that two people who care for each other touched in some ways that made them both feel desired, desirable, safe, and content. This type of intimacy takes patience, communication, caring, and understanding. Please note that we say nothing about age. You're never too old.

Chapter 12

Dating Do's, Don'ts, and Dilemmas

"Intimacy means opening the heart,
Sharing many thoughts I think.
Intimacy means opening my arms,
Offering whatever's me.
Intimacy means taking the risk
Of rejection."

—Elaine Fantle Shimberg

PEOPLE WHO THINK IT'S FUN to jump out of airplanes (with parachutes) say that the first jump is the hardest because you really don't know what to expect. Beginning to date again is somewhat like that, especially when you're suddenly single—through divorce, death of a spouse or partner, or a breakup of a long-term relationship. The thought of dating may seem like an ordeal, ranking right up there with root canals and kidney stones. But attitude is everything, and when you convince yourself you're ready, you can jump in and have fun. Best of all, you control the parachute to let yourself down easily.

A Rose by Any Other Name . . .

Let's face it. For many people, just the word "dating" is enough to cause chills. It conjures up memories from high school and college, of blind dates that didn't work out, of feeling awkward, lonely, and sure that no one else in the world felt as uncomfortable as you about dating. You may think of dating as a young person's activity and feel that you're as far from that as understanding how to program a VCR, operate TiVo, or use the ATM.

But the difficulty isn't with the process as much as the meaning you perceive in the word "dating." So, don't use that word. It's not a very good one anyway because one of the definitions is "to show the age of"! Instead, call it "meeting new friends." That sounds far less threatening and, as William Shakespeare said, it will "smell as sweet."

Even if you aren't sure if you're ready to date, you certainly are ready to meet new friends, aren't you? You'll be surprised how something as simple as changing the name of something can change your attitude. Few people would order "Patagonian toothfish" on a restaurant menu, for example, but under its new name, "Chilean sea bass," it's a popular item.

The First Rendezvous

You meet someone you really enjoy at a party your friend gave, at a lecture series, or, perhaps, you worked with this individual on a community cleanup day where the two of you were part of a team assigned to pick up trash in a public park. Now it seems that he or she had fun being with you and has taken the next step and asked you out for lunch. What should you do?

Well, you do have to eat lunch and it's a good way to get to know someone else better without worrying about how to call it a night if you aren't enjoying yourself. That's why many first dates are for coffee, lunch, or other daytime activities. Go ahead and say yes. Then, if things go well, the next meeting could be for dinner, theater, a movie, or dancing. Don't focus on this being a date or wondering if this relationship will go anywhere. There's no hurry. Enjoy the moment and the opportunity to get to know this friend better. That's why we suggest you think in terms of making a friend and not simply having a new date.

What Do You Talk About?

Many people who are great conversationalists are surprised to discover that they clam up on a first date even when they really enjoy being with the individual. That's usually because they're thinking of this person in light of a possible relationship rather than as a friend. There's nothing wrong with being honest and saying, "This feels a little strange to me. I haven't dated in years." Chances are the other person will open up and tell you how awkward it was when he or she began dating again, too.

To get over this hurdle, get to know your new friend better. Ask questions you'd ask of any new acquaintance. How long have you worked in your present field? What kind of movies or theater do you like? What are your favorite leisuretime activities? You may find that the other person climbs mountains, hikes, and loves camping while you enjoy watching football games, reading, and art galleries. It doesn't mean you'll have to end the friendship; it merely means you both have different interests.

Don't just shoot the questions out one after another without listening to the answers. This meeting is supposed to be a give-and-take conversation period, not a quiz show or monologue. Focus on your companion rather than looking around the room to see if there's anyone else more interesting.

Notice How the Other Person Acts

You also will become aware of subtle clues about this individual. How does he or she treat the waiter or waitress? Are there table manner problems that might be a turnoff, such as talking with a full mouth, putting elbows on the table, or picking at the food on the plate? One man, who had come from a large family, shocked his date when he reached over and speared a piece of tomato off her plate. When he noticed her expression, he apologized, explaining that in his family, trying someone else's food was fair game.

Don't sit there as your date pours down drink after drink, makes sexual advances, or is abusive to you or to others around you. If you find that your date's behavior is actually making you uncomfortable or frightened, you can always leave. Don't worry about being rude or being a spoilsport. Stay in control. It's your parachute. You can always call a taxi if you have a cell phone or ask the manager of the restaurant to call one for you. Never get into the car with someone who's been drinking heavily or shows anger or violent behavior.

What to Do If You Just Want to "Stay Friends"

You may enjoy the other's company and want to spend more time with that person, but really believe the relationship won't go any further than that. You may sense, however, that your friend wants to be more than friends. The best way to handle this type of situation is gently and honestly. Don't just stop seeing someone, leaving him or her wondering what went wrong. Instead, explain that you enjoy being with that person and think of him or her as a good friend, but—and there's always that but—you don't see the relationship going any further. It may cause the other person pain and disappointment, but at least that person can never say you weren't honest and that you led him or her on. As you begin to meet new people and make new friends, always allow those individuals who want more from the relationship than you do to keep their dignity intact; show them respect by offering to remain friends. You can never have too many friends. Then, it's up to the others to determine whether or not to continue the friendship.

Protect Yourself from Emotional and Physical Dangers

There are, of course, dangers other than getting your feelings hurt when you begin to date again. Sexually transmitted diseases (STDs) are not the only risks you can encounter when you begin a new relationship. The difficulties are many. First of all, how do you meet someone and, once you do, protect yourself (physically and emotionally) from getting hurt, while at the same time open yourself to possibilities? Although some of the suggestions that follow apply equally to both men and women, women often are the most vulnerable.

Here are ten rules to remember when you begin to date:

1. Remain alert as you meet new people. That doesn't mean you shouldn't trust anyone you meet, but use common sense. Trust your instincts. If someone makes you uneasy, don't go out with him or her.
2. Don't give out your address to someone you just met.
3. Have your first few dates in public places or double date with friends you know.
4. Don't wear expensive jewelry, flash a wad of bills, or talk about your second home, Lexus, stock portfolio, or the difficulty today in finding good help. Consider finances the "F word" in a new relationship and don't mention it.
5. Carry your cell phone with you and always have enough cash on hand so you can pay for a taxi, if necessary.

6. Minimize your use of alcohol on the first few dates and never use illegal drugs.
7. Never invite a new date to your home until you've dated awhile and feel comfortable. If you want to invite him or her to your home for dinner, invite another couple to join you.
8. Never leave someone new alone with your children or grandchildren until you spend a great deal more time together.
9. Strive for a friendship first.
10. Never get talked into having sex before you're ready, and when you are, *always* practice safe sex.

You Need to Come Out of Hiding

In order to begin dating, you have to make yourself available, to see and be seen, and for many of us, that's a tough requirement. "I'm not a bar hopper," is a refrain we've heard often as though that's the only place to find new faces. Previous chapters have given some specifics on safe places to find people you might like to know better, but if you don't take advantage of them, you might as well be a hermit. It's hard to cross the bridge into "availability," but if you want to meet and enjoy the company of others, that's the territory you need to enter. Part of your success will depend on how well you can focus on simply having fun and meeting new people rather than holding everyone up to the "possible relationship" measure. So, take the classes or seminars that interest you and study the material, not your fellow classmates. If you're excited about what you're learning, you'll seem more alive and interesting than if you take a course just to find somebody. It's the secret of happiness: It finds you when you're not desperately seeking it.

Years ago, when Ellen was in junior high school, she went to the Monday night Y-teen dances—but hid in the ladies' room all evening. When she got home, she confessed to her mother that no one had asked her to dance. She was too young to realize that while hiding out where the boys couldn't find her, she certainly did prevent herself from being a wallflower if boys walked by without asking her to dance, but she also was making it impossible for a young man to find her.

Yet many of us adults are still hiding out when we begin dating again later in life, feeling as awkward as we did in junior high school. While we probably don't go as far as hiding in the bathroom, we hide our emotions and true personalities, trying too hard to impress the person we're with, rather than allowing that person to see us as we are, warts and all.

Some Don'ts for Dating

There are some other "thou shalt nots" of dating that we'll describe here, with specific suggestions on how to circumvent them. While it's true that what doesn't work for one person may be the perfect entrée for another, the results of the following quiz may give you some surprising answers:

DISCOVERING EARLY DATING DON'TS QUIZ

	Yes	No
DO YOU:		
1. Have a tendency to "tell all" about your past, troubles, etc.?	❐	❐
2. Brag about your accomplishments to build self-confidence?	❐	❐
3. Monopolize the conversation?	❐	❐

4. Mentally relive past failures?	❑	❑
5. Let your mind wander as the other talks?	❑	❑
6. Speak too loudly?	❑	❑
7. Smoke?	❑	❑
8. Chew and speak with your mouth open?	❑	❑
9. Talk about your money or lack of it?	❑	❑
10. Show dislike for the plans made by others?	❑	❑
11. Drink excessively?	❑	❑
12. Interrupt often?	❑	❑
13. Lack eye contact?	❑	❑
14. Cling too much; are you overly attentive to the point of seeming needy?	❑	❑

If you have answered yes to two or more questions, you may be chasing away a prospective companion even before he or she ever has the chance to get to know you.

Let's take these points one by one and see why they may turn others off.

1. *Do you chatter a lot?* If you have the tendency to unload on someone you've just met, telling the person about your background, your past, your troubles, misfortunes, misunderstandings, and so on, it may be nervous chatter on your part. But this type of constant chatter may cause a newcomer to back away, thinking you've got too much baggage, unless he or she has a tremendous need to be needed—in which case, *you* may want to back away. When you feel yourself chattering away, stop, close your mouth, and open it only to say, "But tell me about yourself."

2. *Do you brag?* If you find yourself bragging about your accomplishments, you may be trying to boost your self-confidence, but this soon drives others away, which, in turn, lowers your self-esteem. While there's nothing wrong about

telling what you do and showing pride in your accomplishments, guard against giving a dissertation on all your credits and
abilities. Use your successes to see if your new acquaintance
possibly shares your interest. If you both enjoy tennis, for
example, stress that joint interest and see what develops—a
friendly game, doubles, or even a few hints on how to improve
your serve.

3. *Do you monopolize the conversation?* There's a wonderful
country-western song in which the male vocalist says he doesn't
mind listening to her talking about everything that's important to
her, but sometimes he just wants to talk about himself. We all do.
It's perfectly normal. It's called sharing, and when you're single
and searching for someone, it's called being smart.

4. *Do you exhibit knee-jerk reactions?* You may unconsciously find yourself reliving past hurts or failures while you're
trying to get to know someone you've just met. That causes you
to react in the old ways from the past, a knee-jerk reaction that
confuses the other person who has no idea why something he or
she said or did got such a rise out of you. Try to put the past
behind you. Remind yourself that this new person is not the
same one who hurt or rejected you. Because you can't think two
thoughts at once, stop the negative tapes in your head, and
you'll be better able to focus on the positive and perhaps make
a good friend.

5. *Do you tell the person you're not interested without even
saying a word?* While you may not be enthralled instantly when
you begin to talk to a new person, don't let your eyes or mind
wander. This type of body language says plainly, "I'm not interested in you. I'm looking for something better." If your mind
wanders to work you need to do or something else that needs
attention, admit it to the other person honestly and make more of
an effort to be engaged in the conversation. If that's not possible,
then accept that this isn't a good time to talk and say good-bye,

but realize that you may be saying good-bye to someone who could have become a good friend—or more. By explaining that you're in the middle of a deadline at work or wondering if your adult kids got home from their car trip, you may find the other person admitting that he or she has the same concerns and, presto, you have something in common!

6. *Do you speak too loudly?* While it may be that you have a hearing problem, it also may just be a habit you've gotten into. The other person's body language can give you a hint. If he or she is pulling away from you, chances are you're talking too loudly. If people nearby seem to be eavesdropping, that also is a clue that you need to lower the volume of your conversation. If you think you might have hearing problems, seek out an audiologist or an otolaryngologist (ear, nose, and throat specialist). You could simply have wax in your ears or another condition that can be corrected.

7. *Are you a smoker?* That can be deadly, especially if the other person isn't a smoker. If you've asked if he or she minds and you get an okay, remember to be thoughtful and not hold the cigarette so the smoke blows in the other person's face. Better yet, don't smoke. Of course, if you both smoke, then this is a nonissue for dating.

8. *Do you chew with your mouth open?* How would you know? One clue: If you have trouble with abdominal gas, you might be swallowing air as you eat. It's very unpleasant to sit opposite another person who chews this way. If you speak with food in your mouth, you may be a spitter, which means as you speak, you're spitting tiny morsels of food across the table. The other person is faced with being obvious and wiping the food off his or her clothes or face or sitting there wishing you were anywhere else. Talking with food in your mouth is a good way to assure that the first date is the last date.

9. *Do you talk about your money or lack of it?* This isn't a

good idea, especially when you're just meeting someone. It could turn others off or actually be dangerous as someone might want to steal from you. Don't wear expensive jewelry on your first few dates or talk about your second home in the mountains or on the beach. While it's okay today to split a check, don't lend money to someone you don't know too well. (Actually, you're better off never loaning money. That's what banks are for.) Also, don't be a "pity poor me," talking about how you can't afford to buy nice clothes, to travel, or to have a nicer home. Your date may consider you high maintenance and say "thanks, but no thanks."

10. *Do you show dislike for plans that are made?* Do you complain the movie isn't the one you wanted to see, you hate Chinese food, and you find bowling a bore? If you don't get your way, do you pout or refuse to play? Better to be a good sport and try something new. Griping and moaning are good ways to end a relationship before it ever starts.

11. *Do you drink alcohol excessively?* Try to slow down, because heavy drinkers tend to say and do foolish things. Some experts suggest that you should never drink on a first date, then drink only moderately on subsequent dates. If you believe you might have a drinking problem, consider going to an AA meeting.

12. *Do you interrupt often?* When we interrupt, we usually do so because we want to interject an idea and are afraid we'll forget it. But what we're actually saying is "I don't think what you're saying is that important, so listen to me." It's a bad habit and one that can be very irritating to others. If you tend to interrupt, think before you speak and be sure the other person is finished.

13. *Do you avoid eye contact?* If so, this gives the impression that you're either very bored or quite unsure of yourself, unless you're from a culture where eye contact isn't polite. You don't have to stare at the other person, but looking down at the table

or at a dust spot on your sleeve or making designs in spilled sugar on the tablecloth doesn't make the other person feel too important. How would you like it?

14. *Are you clinging? Overattentive?* Women like to receive compliments and gifts, but don't overdo it or the attention loses its importance. The same goes for men. They also like to hear good things about themselves, but don't be a gusher.

Do these fourteen points mean you have to be perfect in every way when you meet someone new? Not at all. No one's perfect. Not you and not the other person. Remember that not even Mother Nature is perfect. It's said that no two snowflakes are alike, yet each is beautiful. Find that beauty in your companion.

Chapter 13

Dealing with Adult Children and Grandchildren

"Genuine appreciation of other people's
children is one of the rarer virtues."

—Harlan Miller, American journalist

YOU PROBABLY HAVEN'T GIVEN much thought about the issue of
children, at least not at this point in your life. When you meet
someone new and enjoy being with him or her, it's natural to
assume that a new relationship will be between only you and
the other person. Yet if either of you has children or grandchildren, it's important to consider the impact these family members
can have on your lives and your budding relationship. And if
you thought the terrible twos were difficult, you ain't seen
nothing yet!

When Should You Tell the Kids?

Assuming that your children are teenagers or adults, you should
let them know as soon as you believe a friendship is beginning
to have more serious feelings. You don't have to go into details,
other than saying, "I really care a great deal for Joan. I'm anxious
for you to meet her," or "I have fun with Sam. I'd like to invite

him over for one of our family barbecues." Be willing to answer any questions, such as "Are you thinking of getting married again?" or "Are you moving in together?" and reassure your kids that you're going slow in order to get to know the other person better, and if the answer to their questions would ever become yes, you'll let them know.

Introduce them to your companion early in your growing relationship. It isn't fair to suddenly bring someone to Thanksgiving dinner and announce you're thinking of moving in together. Even if the relationship fizzles, at least you've reminded your kids that you're still in the market for a special friend.

Sally disagreed with this advice: "I hadn't dated anyone with kids until I met my late husband, in my late forties. My advice would be to let the relationship really evolve for quite awhile (months, not weeks) before getting involved with them. I was lucky in that they wanted their dad to be happy and we got serious fairly quickly, but in the endgame, they reverted to Mom and left me bereft of both my husband, when he died, and my "extended" family after twelve years of marriage. You'd better be prepared for how you feel about sharing a guy's time and resources with others who have just come into your life."

But none of us can predict how life turns out and by putting up too many defenses, you might be locking out many years of companionship and love. Be willing to take some risks, but go slowly so you can move out of harm's way if you begin to feel uncomfortable with a relationship.

Usually, if your kids don't feel left out and they know you're not rushing into a situation, they'll be more content. Two adult sisters, Kayla and Susan, felt immediate antagonism to their sixty-four-year-old mother's new boyfriend, not just because he was twenty-five years younger and unemployed, but because he moved in with their mother a week after the two had met. The mistake here was that their mother moved entirely too fast for the sisters to believe she was making a good decision. "The age thing didn't bother me," Susan said, "as much as the fact that she didn't get to know him well enough before having him move in." So take your time.

Concerns of Adult Children

If you're dating someone with children or grandchildren, you may find a positive reaction to your relationship from them. However, you may find those "kids" try to protect their turf—wanting to keep things the way they were before you came onto the scene. This turf protecting may include rudeness, lying about something you or your new prospective partner may have said, or just refusing to be in the same room with you. Chalk up these behaviors to jealousy and a fear of losing their parent's love. Do such behaviors sound more like a child's reaction than a mature adult's? While it may be a childish reaction, it's also natural. Take Sam, for example, whose partner's college-age children were rude to him in the beginning. "My partner had gotten divorced," he said. "I think in many ways that's harder on children, adult or not, than if a parent dies. Her kids were suspicious. One asked if I was going to leave her mother, too."

Naturally, in such situations you feel as though you're caught in the middle. And you are. But by understanding why kids react the way they do, you can do much to help ease relations between your new partner and the adult children whom either of you bring to the relationship.

Here are some issues that children of any age tend to find difficult to handle:

- *Death of a parent*. If your spouse is deceased, your adult children may feel you're being disloyal to his or her memory.

Not that they want you to melt into the rocking chair on the porch, but they find it difficult to see you wanting to share your life with someone new. "Why can't you just be happy with us?" is often the unasked question. One widower confided that, although his adult children liked his new partner, one of them said to him, "You've got lots of pictures of Lucille around, but there's no picture of Mom." He quickly added a family photo that included a picture of his late wife.

• *Jealousy.* Whether you're divorced or widowed, part of your children's resentment is jealousy, not wanting to share you with someone else. And, to be honest, part of it may be resentment that you'll be spending some of your money (and their inheritance) with a "stranger."

• *You're not acting your age.* If the person you've found is considerably younger than you, your family may harbor concerns that the individual is a gold digger who's trying to steal your money. Parents, in their minds, should act their age, and it goes without saying, also in their minds, parents should act their age only with others of the same age group.

• *You're sexually active.* Your adult kids may find it difficult to believe that sex is still an important part of your life, and they certainly don't want to picture you as a sexual being (as they are). It's somewhat akin to their denial as kids when you first told them the facts of life. When a medical writer spoke to a group of medical students, she described how they need to listen to their older patients and ask them specific questions on relationship issues including their sexual life. "You may be surprised to learn," she told the students, "that your parents are still 'doing it' and there's a good likelihood that your grandparents are, too." The medical students began giggling. "Absurd idea," they said to each other.

The key to overcoming the objections of your children or your partner's children is to keep the lines of communication open, especially in cases where the adult children are rejecting or downright hostile. You may be surprised to discover that adult kids won't necessarily welcome a new potential partner in their parent's life even though their parent's divorce may have taken place many years ago. The new partner may still be considered an intruder, especially if their other parent hasn't found anyone and is still alone. But you can often soften their responses. One seventy-year-old man who was in an intimate relationship with a woman his age told the woman's adult son, "I know you don't like me that much, but let's be polite for your mother's sake because I know you love her." That cleared the air and although the two didn't become close buddies, they at least could be civil to one another at family gatherings. And that type of politeness should be insisted upon. Overt rudeness has no place in mature adult relationships.

How to Become a Sudden Stepparent

Tread carefully. These "kids" are adults in their own right, have jobs, vote, and may have their own children. While you may feel you're an expert in what's wrong with other people's children, bite your tongue. Never tell your partner what his or her adult children are doing wrong either in their lives or in raising their own children. Your partner may feel the need to defend them (although silently agreeing with your opinion) and suddenly you'll find yourself in the middle.

In *Blending Families*, I (Elaine) write about ways to build a successful new family. While these building blocks are important in laying the foundation for family members living under one roof (some of them only part time because of joint custody), they are equally important when you suddenly find yourself a "stepparent" (or a partner-parent) to adult children who don't live with you, but still have a close relationship with their parent. Here are some suggestions for successfully building a good relationship with these children:

Don't Overwhelm Them with Gifts or By Being Overly Friendly

They'll see through you in a heartbeat if you constantly come bearing gifts and act overly friendly. These are adults, but important ones to your partner. Be courteous, friendly, and interested in them, their children, and their activities. If you're lucky and they ask you about yourself (through curiosity, true interest, or grilling to make sure you're not a serial killer or child abuser), answer truthfully and briefly without monopolizing the conversation. You're a stranger in their territory and they need time to get used to you. Let them come to you without your being stand-offish or acting disinterested.

Know When to Keep Your Mouth Shut

If you find yourself in a family grouping at Christmas, Thanksgiving, Passover, or birthdays, don't chatter nervously. Ask if you can help clear or wash the dishes, but be a good listener. Don't brag or try to sell yourself, because you'll come across as "too pushy." Be careful about agreeing if they criticize their parent, even in fun. If you agree, they may take your words seriously and quote them to your partner. The wrong words can damage your relationship with your partner's adult children and, if quoted inaccurately or even accurately, can harm your relationship with your partner.

Never Criticize Your Partner's Ex-Spouse—Ever—
to His or Her Kids

It should go without saying. They'll react faster than bees swarming all over you and you'll wish you had held your tongue. Inspirational writer Robert Fulghum was correct when he wrote: "Sticks and stones may break my bones, but words will break our hearts."

Let Them Know You Have No Intention (or Need)
to Take Their Other Parent's Place

This is an important point to make even though you're dealing with grown-up children. They need to be assured that, although you want a relationship with their parent, you have no intention of trying to take their other parent's place, regardless if that parent is deceased or divorced. Let your partner's adult children know that you would like to be friends with them because you love your partner and know that family is an important part of his or her life.

Let Them Know You Care for and Respect Their Parent

Even if his or her kids don't want you in their parent's life, they'll feel better if you quietly and without fanfare let them know that you love, respect, and care for their parent. You can do it subtly, as simply as saying, "Your dad (or mom) is very special to me. You're lucky to have had him (her) for a father (mother)." Then prove it by not telling tales when they joke about his or her foibles.

Refrain from Public Displays of Affection

While a pat on the arm or even hand-holding is okay in

front of his or her kids, refrain from public displays of affection such as nibbling on the neck, stroking a leg, or other suggestive acts. All kids—adult and younger—have difficulty picturing a parent being sexual. You'll stir up too many emotions that may be expressed as dislike for you. Save your physical tenderness for your more private moments.

Stay Out of Money Discussions Between Your Partner and His or Her Kids

You may (rightly) feel that your partner gives too much money to his or her kids and that they take advantage of the generosity. This is an argument you can't win because there's too much emotion involved. If your partner is divorced from the kids' other parent, there may be a great deal of guilt floating around in the air. Money is often used to settle some of that guilt down.

Learn How to Handle Family Holidays and Other Family Get-togethers

"Home for the holidays" might have been part of a good song title, but it can certainly cause discord when a newcomer joins the mix. You may have always had Christmas dinner or Passover at your home and your adult kids look forward to coming over with their families. Of course you want to include the new someone in your life because the holiday is special to you. So what should you do? Begin by telling your family that this person is important to you and you want him or her to meet your family (if that hasn't already happened). Don't let it be a surprise when "Santa" or "Elijah" walks in.

If you've always been included at one of your children's homes for a holiday, privately tell your child that you'd like to invite a guest who is important in your life. Or try another option as Harry and Florence did. Harry, age seventy-two, and Florence, sixty-one, were married in January. When their first Christmas came up, they weren't sure what to do because each had always spent Christmas with their respective adult children. They solved their dilemma by going away together, just the two of them.

Blending Families Doesn't Always Mix Smoothly

Realize that there are what Dorian Solot and Marshall Miller, authors of *Unmarried to Each Other*, call "tribal differences." Your new partner's family may have certain customs and traditions that seem foreign or "wrong" to you. It may be as simple as their eating on paper plates at family gatherings while you always use your best china and silver, or opening all the Christmas presents Christmas Eve while your family waits until Christmas morning.

Solot and Miller point to the difference in spending choices, where one family seeks out the best deals while the other always goes first class, buying the finest wines and gourmet cheeses. "Recognizing that many differences are not based on different morals, values, or opinions, but rather different *tribes* can save you a lot of arguing."

Recognizing tribal differences can keep you from being critical when you see your partner's adult kids doing things far different from what you taught your own kids. It reminds you that you and your partner will have differences as well, and if your relationship continues, you'll have to determine if it's really worth arguing over whether you use the very last bit of toothpaste in the tube or toss it, buy brand names at the grocery rather than generic, or put the toilet paper roll in the holder so the paper comes over the top or up from the bottom. Just say to yourself, "It must be a tribal thing," and enjoy your relationship.

Peter K. Gerlach, who writes articles and offers information on his Web site (*http://sfhelp.org*), says: "The odds of significant one-time or ongoing conflict between stepparents and adult stepkids—and secondary conflicts with spouses, ex-mates, and biochildren—are higher than casual observers think. The core conflicts are just the same as with younger stepsons and step-daughters and the environment is very different."

We claim that you don't have to be married for this phenomenon to occur because the same is true in any dating relationship that is deemed threatening by adult children. The adult stepchild (or what we call, "partner stepchild") doesn't feel any obligation to be nice to you as the "new guy in town" because he or she is grown up and you aren't helping to raise him or her. What's more, these adult stepchildren may have their own kids to raise and don't need to spend all their efforts sparring with you.

Peter Gerlach lists a number of problems with adult stepchildren that he's familiar with in his practice. We altered some of them slightly to reflect a special friendship or relationship in progress, rather than a marriage:

- You feel personally disrespected, ignored, or lied to, too much, too often.
- You disrespect, distrust, or dislike an adult stepchild and/or his or her children.
- You distrust the judgment of a grown stepchild and fear he or she will make decisions that will harm him- or herself and any kids, and cause major stress in your relationship.
- You resent the way your partner's adult child treats your partner.
- You resent or disrespect your partner for not asserting

what you feel are proper boundaries with his or her grown children or ex-mate.

- You worry about the welfare of an adult stepchild and feel he or she needs professional help.
- You feel trapped in battles between your own adult kids and your partner's adult kids, or resent your partner's grown kids disrespecting, ignoring, or using your adult kids or grandkids.
- You feel excessive guilt at the way you feel about or treat one of your partner's grown children.
- You honestly don't like one of your partner's kids and really don't want to spend time with him or her.
- You can't talk or problem-solve with your partner about issues like these.

What to Do If There's a Problem with an Adult Stepchild

Many issues you face are communication problems. Feeling frustrated or angry won't solve anything and can actually make the problems worse. Instead, take a deep breath and follow these suggestions:

1. *Make time to sit quietly with your partner and urge him or her to discuss whatever difficulties you're facing.* Turn off the TV and let the answering machine take any phone messages.

2. *Let your partner know that you're bothered with these problems.* Communicate that you both need to find solutions if your relationship is to work.

3. *Discuss the problem unemotionally.* First, you speak, and then your partner, with neither of you interrupting the other.

4. *Agree that you will respect one another's adult children and grandchildren* (regardless if you like them or not).

5. *Consider if you have ill feelings because the adult kid*

you're having difficulties with reminds you of someone you disliked in your past. Is he or she becoming a scapegoat for you?

6. *Examine your mutual expectations.* Do you agree that you and your partner can have a relationship without both of your families becoming best friends with each other, as long as they respect one another? You may have been unconsciously trying to merge families so you all are "one big happy family." Remember that you both come from different tribes.

7. *Try to communicate with the adult stepchild honestly, but respectfully.* Perhaps this will open conversation so the adult partner stepchild can answer, "You'll never take my father's (or mother's) place." Then you can readily agree and try to develop a friendship based on mutual respect. In fact, to ward off antagonism from the beginning, ask the adult kids to call you by your first name so they immediately know that you aren't trying to become another "Mom" or "Dad." (The stepgrandkids will probably come up with their own name for you. It could be as simple as "Grandma Two" or "Papa George.")

How to Handle the Ex-Spouse

You may find yourself having to socialize at times with your partner's ex-spouse, especially if there are weddings, christenings, bar or bas mitzvahs, or other life-cycle events. Be civil and friendly, even if the ex-spouse seems cool to you at first. You can afford to be charitable. After all, you are now in your partner's life. And who knows, you may actually find yourself enjoying the ex-spouse's company at these events.

Think Twice Before You Move into Your Partner's House

It often is very upsetting to adult children to see a new woman in their mother's former home, especially if their mother is deceased. You will probably want to make a few changes in décor, and these changes will be seen as criticism of their poor dead mother. And, one of them is bound to ask, "What's going to happen to my mother's china, silver, and our great-grandmother's desk that's been in the family?" To keep the peace, it's usually better to move into a new home, apartment, or condo that is memory-free for both you and your partner, to use your things, and to let the adult children lay claim to possessions that once were their mother's. (And the truth is, you might prefer having your own things, rather than feeling you were a guest in the ghost wife's home.)

Men don't usually feel as uncomfortable in another man's former home, but before he moves in with you, this is definitely a discussion that needs to take place. Once again, it may be better to find a place that is uniquely yours to keep your adult kids from snarling if a new man is ensconced in "Dad's favorite chair."

Maintain Contact with Your Own Adult Kids

Recognize that your adult children may want to have time alone with you without the new partner around. It's the same feeling many parents have, desiring to spend time alone with their own child without always having the child's spouse there, but not wanting to hurt any feelings by saying so. Be sensitive to this issue and plan times that you can be alone with your adult child—playing golf, shopping, having lunch, and so on. Also encourage your partner to spend some "quality time" with his adult kids and grandkids as well, without you in the picture. If you play your cards right, one of them may say, "Where's your lady friend? Why didn't you bring her?"

Open communication is important so that you or your adult child can call each other and feel comfortable saying, "I'd love to spend some time alone with you. How about . . ." It doesn't mean you don't love your new partner. It just means we all need to spend time with others, especially others we also love very much.

Chapter 14

To Live Together or Live Apart?

"'Mid pleasures and palaces though we may roam,
Be it ever so humble, there's no place like home."

—John Howard Payne (1791–1852),
from the opera *Clari, the Maid of Milan*

WHILE IT'S PROBABLY TRUE that there's no place like home, when
you've been dating the same person for awhile and your relationship seems to be going well, the question often arises,
"Should we move in together?" And that question is closely followed by, "If so, where?" How do you decide whether or not
to move in together? And if you decide to do so, when should
you do it?

As with many decisions within a relationship, there are no
clear-cut rules, because each relationship is unique. There are,
however, some common questions that every couple needs to
consider and answer before making this decision. Why? Because
moving out when it becomes obvious that a mistake has been
made is a great deal harder emotionally, physically, financially,
and in every other way than moving in. There are no right or
wrong answers to these questions. Rather, your answers indicate
which issues need to be discussed and where you should seek
compromise if you have differences. Ask yourself and your
partner why you both want to live together. Is it . . .

- To save money?
- To have help running a home?
- To keep from being lonely?
- To grow old(er) together?
- To determine if we want to marry?
- To make it easier to have sex?
- To keep the kids from worrying about your being alone?
- To have someone to talk to (besides the cat)?
- To let others know we're a couple?

A good book to help you further determine whether or not you should consider cohabitation is *Unmarried to Each Other* by Dorian Solot and Marshall Miller. Don't think you're unique if you decide to move in together. According to the U.S. Census Bureau: "20 percent of those between forty-five to sixty live together without being married." And, it's not just the middle-age folks, either. Armas Genaro, in an article titled "Census: More Elderly Live Together" (Associated Press, July 30, 2002), wrote: "Between 1990 and 2000, the number of senior citizens cohabitors tripled."

Power of the "M" word

There is a tremendous power in the "M" word, which in this case does not stand for "marriage," but rather "move in." When the subject comes up about the possibility of one of you moving in with the other, it immediately puts your relationship on a decidedly different level. It represents a significant step (at least on the part of one person and, hopefully, both of you) and a desire for the relationship to remain permanent. Think carefully about yours and your partner's motivation for moving in together. Of course, the "right" and "wrong" reasons differ from relationship to relationship.

Following is a list of common motivations for moving in together. Look it over carefully, and be sure that you are comfortable with both yours and your partner's motivations for taking that step.

- You both want to save on rent or mortgage payments, which could be especially important if you both are on a fixed income.
- You're interested in downsizing, especially if both of you still have big houses where you raised your families.
- You'd like to be available to take care of each other, which could be especially important if one or both of you have chronic illnesses such as asthma or arthritis and would feel more comfortable having someone else in the home in case of an emergency.
- You just want the convenience of being together so you can enjoy each other's companionship.
- You both feel it's time to move your relationship along to a more permanent feeling, even if neither of you wants to marry.
- You both want to show your commitment to each other to your friends and family members so they begin to think of you as a couple.
- You both have a desire to relieve loneliness that may arise from living alone.
- You both are interested in being able to enjoy spontaneous sex rather than having to plan for it.
- You both feel it's time to establish "our" home, rather than "your home" and "my home."

You're Moving in Together—Now Come the Big Decisions

Once you've determined that you will move in together, there are a number of other factors to consider and questions to ask and mutual decisions to make:

- *Where will you move?* Will it be your present home? Your partner's present home? A new home? In the same town? A different town? In the city? In the country?
- *Who keeps what furniture?* If you're Swedish modern and your partner has nineteenth-century English antiques, and you have special favorite pieces, you both may have to make some concessions. Perhaps you can each have a room to decorate.
- *What will you do with all the "stuff" you've accumulated over the years?* What will happen to the family photos, college memorabilia, collections, coffee mugs, trophies, plaques, and so on?
- *Who will care for the family pets, if any?* People love their pets and become emotional about them, so this could be a difficult decision if one of you doesn't like animals or is allergic. While your partner is important, try to make a decision that is also considerate of the pet. If you have to part with Spot or Tabby, be sure you've found a good home rather than just someone who says, "okay." If your pet is an older animal, you may not want to place it in a home with small children. If you're really uncertain whether to give away a pet or end a relationship, take a good look at the relationship. There may be problems you haven't acknowledged before.
- *Are your living habits compatible, at least to a degree?* As most of us are, you're probably a little set in your ways. But if you're a compulsive housekeeper who washes towels every day and throws out the newspaper by noon and your partner is one who tosses sweaty tennis clothes on the floor and never wipes

the toothpaste out of the sink, tempers may fly. Be sure you can live with each other's living habits regardless how much in love you may be.

• *Who pays for what?* Do you equally share the rent or mortgage payment or does the person with the larger income pay more? Who pays for the Direct TV, the Internet access, the newspaper, groceries, and appliance repairs? What about the telephone long distance if one of you has three adult kids who live out of town and the other only has two? Discuss your finances before you share a home together so there's no misunderstanding.

• *Who will do what chores?* Will you share cooking and cleanup? Yard work? Laundry? What about other errands such as going to the dry cleaners, taking shoes to be repaired, taking appliances to be repaired, and taking the car to be repaired?

• *How will you deal with any outstanding debts that either of you has incurred?* Are there outstanding bills, credit card charges, alimony payments?

• *How will you decide where to call home?* You live in the city and your partner lives in the country; you live in Tampa and your partner lives in Seattle. How do you decide where to call home? Geographic moves are much more difficult than moving across town because the one who moves to a new community gives up friends; familiar restaurants, stores, physicians, and activities; and in some cases, family. It's sometimes harder to "start over" as you get older. Think about it carefully before either of you agrees to such a major move. Some couples compromise by moving to a neutral spot, a place they may have visited together and enjoyed. That way you make new friends together, as a couple, and no one really cares if you're married or just "cohabiting."

• *Have you really thought about the lack of privacy once you share your living quarters?* Are you willing to make compromises, understanding that things won't be exactly as they have been when you lived alone?

Are You Moving into Your Partner's Home?

Even if both of you are enthusiastic about merging residences, you may find it seems a little strange to be moving into someone else's home. Be sure to discuss ahead of time some of your specific needs so your requirements don't come as a surprise. For example, if you have young grandchildren who are used to having toys to play with when they come to visit, is there a place to store the blocks, games, and dolls so the grandkids will still feel welcomed? If they like spending an overnight with "Grammy" or "Grandpa," is there a spare bedroom, a couch that opens up, or space for a blow-up bed so they can continue this practice? Do you have a hobby or collection that might require some space? Do you want to bring your favorite cookware, dishes, tools, or large items such as a bike, grill, or entertainment center?

What pieces of furniture do you want to bring with you? A realistic touch in the television show *Frazier* is the tattered recliner chair that Frazier's father brought with him when he moved into Frazier's modern condo. We all have special pieces of furniture—a desk that was our grandmother's, an end table our son made in high school shop class, or a pair of Waterford lamps that were a wedding present from our parents. Just as a toddler needs his or her favorite sleep toy in order to bed down without a fuss, we all have our comfort pieces that we need to make us feel "at home."

Would you like to see a makeover in the decorating in your partner's home? It may be as minor as subtly suggesting a more soothing paint color instead of the orange and blue or as major as redoing the second bedroom so you'd have a study/library and a place to use your computer.

Discuss these changes *before* you move in, in order to make your partner's home your home as well. Don't spring it one morning at breakfast after you've already taken up residency. Also, ask for a complete inventory and tour of your partner's home so you don't have to keep asking, "How does the heat turn on?" or "Where do you keep the spare lightbulbs?" The more comfortable you feel about his or her house, the more quickly it will feel like home to you.

And finally, if you're moving into your partner's home, be sure your partner reads this next section. It will help your partner think about how to make your move more comfortable.

Is Your Partner Moving into Your Home?

Although you may be very excited at the thought of having your partner move in with you, remember that, although you know every nook and cranny, the home may be a little foreign to him or her at first. Give a tour, showing where you store the extra air conditioning filters, where you put your luggage, and how the built-in vacuum system and satellite television works.

Clean out a few closets and dressers, too, so that there is ample room for your partner's possessions. It's probably a good excuse for you to go through things and toss those you've outgrown or just don't wear anymore. Thin out the coat closet, too, so there's room for your partner's jackets, coats, and rain gear.

Discuss ahead of the move what furniture you are willing to store so there's room for his or her favorites. If you have grown kids, they might be pleased to have some of your chairs, end tables, or lamps. Don't be upset if they don't want them, however. Personal taste differs, even in close families. If you don't want to pay for storing pieces you can't use, give them to a thrift shop or a store that pays you a (small) percent of what it sells them for.

Create space in your kitchen, bathroom, and even your

bookshelves so your partner can move in some of his or her personal things. Be willing to free up some wall space for his or her special paintings, too. Welcoming these familiar touches makes a newcomer feel more at home as a permanent resident and less like a temporary boarder. Isn't that what you want?

Expect to Make Some Adjustments

Keep communication open so each of you can freely express your feelings and needs. Living together, regardless of how much time you have spent with each other, including numerous "sleepovers," can create unexpected issues, but moving in together need not be a traumatic experience. By talking about your expectations, you can head off arguments, hurt feelings, and disappointment.

Each of you may have previously lived alone for a period of time. It's different when there's always someone around. It's a good feeling, but it also limits privacy. You may be used to a lot of thinking or reading time, while your partner loves to chatter about the weather, the world situation, and what's coming up on television. You may not have noticed it before because you weren't always together before this.

If you like to read the paper and drink your coffee before engaging in conversation, say so at the beginning, so your partner doesn't sulk and wonder why you aren't talking. If you like to use the bathroom privately, say so. Otherwise, your partner may barge in, thinking that you like the togetherness. You need to respect each other's preferences, but because neither of you probably are qualified as mind readers, you'll have to voice that information rather than expect your partner to guess how you feel.

It's unlikely that you'll be able to offer a list of "this is what I like and don't like" ahead of time, so agree that you'll quickly speak up if something happens that offends or upsets you. It may be as slight as the *Sports Illustrated* magazines piling up on the coffee table or your partner never replacing a roll of toilet paper when the old roll runs out, but if it bothers you, you need to say so. Otherwise, these issues will pile up like leaves in the drain pipe and you'll eventually be flooded out.

What If You're Not Ready to Share a Home?

It is possible that one of you will utter the "M" word before the other is ready. That can be an awkward moment, but it need not ruin your relationship. By all means, tell your partner why you're hesitating.

It may be that neither of you is ready to change locales. You're a city person and love the convenience of public transportation, the theater, the shops, the fruit stands, that you can buy flowers at all hours during the night, and just the general hubbub and sounds of the city. Moving to the suburbs or to the country would be very hard for you. Your partner, on the other hand, relishes the solitude, the sounds of frogs croaking, the songs of the birds, and the gurgling of the brook. What to do?

If you can afford two homes, a compromise might be to live in the city during the week, but go to the country on the weekend. That would satisfy both your souls, if finances permit. Otherwise, you might have to agree that although you both want your relationship to continue, you both would be happiest living apart, with the city person spending occasional weekends in the country, and the country person coming into the city for certain occasions.

But if locations aren't the problem, and you still don't feel comfortable making the commitment to move in together, then you need to talk. It may be that you're not ready just yet, but want the relationship to continue. Perhaps, if you're honest, it could also be that you don't picture this as the permanent relationship you want for yourself. And lastly, it just may be that you are very happy living alone because you cherish your privacy, but you very much want to continue the relationship. Then, by all means, communicate this to your partner. You might be surprised to learn that he or she is relieved by your decision and is very happy staying put as well and continuing the relationship.

You might find yourself in the same frame of mind as Sam and Lucille. After Sam's second wife died, he decided not to remarry. "I told Lucille on our second date that I didn't want any relationship to result in marriage. Fortunately, she felt the same way. We each have our own homes. I spend one day during the week at hers as I volunteer at a nursing home close to where she lives. She comes to stay with me on Friday, after work. It's really the highlight of my week. I cook for her. I'm excited for her company. It works well for us."

We know of a number of cases where couples travel together, go out for dinner together, and see plays and movies together, but for personal (and very acceptable) reasons prefer to keep their own homes and not move in together. Should you move in together? It seems as though the answer to this question could be a simple yes or no, but actually, it needs much more thought. Consider your decision carefully and base it on reality, not just the emotion and excitement of the moment. Living with another person, as wonderful as it may be, does add additional stress no matter what your age. What's more, most of us tend to get a little set in our ways as we get older. So take your time. It's a big decision and one that has to feel right to both of you. Whatever works!

Chapter 15

If You're Considering
an Alternative Lifestyle

"One of the oldest human needs is having someone to wonder
where you are when you don't come home at night."

—Margaret Mead (1901–1978), anthropologist and writer

SOME INDIVIDUALS WANT TO EXPLORE nontraditional lifestyles—
open marriages, bisexuality, and homosexuality. There's no
question that each of us is different, so it's little wonder that each
of us has different needs, especially in friendships and relationships. What works for one person may be the antithesis of what
another would desire. Yet it makes no sense to try to impose
your needs and wishes on others, but simply to accept the differences. There really is no "right" or "wrong"; it is just the way
we are. Mahatma Gandhi said: "Our besetting sin is not difference, but our littleness." Our only caution is that you read
Chapter 11 for information on sexually transmitted diseases,
which are on the rise, especially among gay males and postmenopausal heterosexual adults.

Open Marriage

If both persons are comfortable with some degree of openness,
then exploration probably can actually enhance the relationship.

But if one wants monogamy and the other wanders, that relationship is doomed. It easily deteriorates into a control issue. Friends don't remain friends when one attempts to control the other.

If you are interested in understanding more about open marriage, read the updated version of *Open Marriage* by Nena and George O'Neil. The book looks at committed, egalitarian relationships and it stresses open, clear communication. According to the authors, couples of all persuasions can enjoy additional intimacies together or apart, but an open relationship demands that both parties give up possessiveness. If you and your partner are interested, you should be very careful to negotiate the terms of your commitments clearly and openly, and you should have this discussion fairly early in your dating relationship. If you know you're not interested in an open marriage and could never be comfortable with such an arrangement, but your partner is equally sure he or she prefers it, you might as well discontinue the relationship before it goes any further.

If you're open to many possibilities, you might enjoy reading *Relating,* the newsletter of the Institute for 21st Century Relationships. Ask for a copy of volume 2, issue 4. You can contact the organization at: 2419 Little Current Drive, Suite 1933, Herndon, Virginia 20171 (703-561-8136) or online at *www. lovethatworks.org.* The philosophy of this organization is . . .

Attaining a satisfactory level of love and companionship through intimate relations is an unalterable, fundamental need of all human beings. The Institute for 21st Century Relationships exists to facilitate the fulfillment of the human potential for relating, and to support the freedom of consenting adults to discover and practice the intimate relationship structure that best meets their emotional and human needs. We champion the basic human right to do so free of governmental, societal, or institutional coercion or favoritism. We seek, through education, research, and support, to create a climate in which all forms of ethical, consensual, and fulfilling relationship styles are broadly understood and are equally respected and honored as legitimate choices . . . Persons participating in an open-ended marriage [solemnly commit to] each other, but [to] the whole Family of Man . . . Within such marriages the possibility of adultery is totally absent because exclusion, possessiveness, and jealousy have no place in the relationship. 'Adultery' is a theological judgment which can only apply to the restrictive type of covenant. When one partner breaks the vow of 'to thee only do I promise to keep myself,' a relationship of trust is broken and he or she is unfaithful. But it's also possible to create a model of marriage—a covenant—monogamous in the sense that it's based upon an intended lifetime commitment between the two but which nevertheless is open-ended because it does not exclude the freedom to have any number of intimate relationships with others.

Is this type of a relationship "right" for everyone? Absolutely not. Might it be something you'd be interested in? Possibly. You have the right to choose what works for you and explore yourself.

On Being Gay, Lesbian, or Bisexual

According to the 2000 Census, there were 1.2 million people who admitted living with a same-sex partner. Most likely, this number is actually larger because many gay, lesbian, and bisexual people may not be ready to "come out" on an official governmental form.

A midlife crisis for some single people over age forty comes when it dawns on them that they've lived half of their expected life span as a lie. Maybe it's been without serious problems until this realization point, but now they want to explore what they believe is their authentic sexual orientation. It may come as a shock to adult children and their grandparents when Mom or Dad, now single, admits that he or she is more comfortable in a lesbian or gay relationship. While much has been written on how to handle the situation when you find your son or daughter is homosexual, less is available for grown kids when Mom or Dad makes the announcement. It's more information about their parent's sexuality than they want to know.

PFLAG, an organization for parents, families and friends of lesbians and gays, offers a variety of reading materials for parents, grandparents, family, and friends. You can contact PFLAG at: 1726 M Street NW, Suite 400, Washington, DC 20036 (202-467-8180), online at *www.pflag.org,* or via e-mail at *info@pflag.org.*

It's Not All About Sex, Regardless of Your Lifestyle

While it's not that difficult for most people to find a sexual partner or to live a promiscuous life experimenting with many partners and encounters, what is difficult is to find a special partner—a best friend, companion, and lover to share your life. Despite hundreds of self-help books, an endless list of exciting psychotherapy techniques, and an explosion in talk-show specials on love and intimacy, people's ability to form lasting and satisfying relationships is still a difficult struggle fraught with repeated failure.

Virtually everyone says that love begins with arousal, with a feeling of attraction, the so-called chemistry of being turned on. While this may be true, there is a very poor correlation between chemistry and success in a relationship. There's no doubt that arousal works. Certainly, a majority of relationships start out this way, but there's absolutely no guarantee that arousal will last, certainly not with the intensity of the opening shot, and people who measure the quality of their relationship based on sexual excitement are usually disappointed. We've often met couples, both gay and heterosexual, who describe themselves as "madly in love," but months later, they're just plain mad.

One of our misjudgments when dealing with human emotions is unwittingly exaggerating the importance of sex. We become confused by unrealistic expectations about what love is supposed to do for us. Lust itself can be a real distraction to an authentic relationship. Not all people start out with chemistry and passion. We know many relationships that have lasted longer than forty years. These began with simple friendships, and over time, the sensuousness evolved, ultimately blossoming into lustful and stable relationships. Marriage? Not always. Not always possible. Often, not legal. A well-known gay author and lecturer maintained a relationship of twenty-five years that started with a simple friendship. There was no real "hot to trot" chemistry in the beginning, but over time, their continuing appreciation and respect for each other grew into a full-scale, erotic, and trusting relationship.

Jim Quinlan, former editor of the *Gay and Lesbian Times* (Palm Springs), posed this question: "Here in our desert paradise, we see hundreds and hundreds of gay and lesbian couples in relationships that appear relatively stable. Many of them have been together for decades, with varying degrees of satisfaction. Some of these relationships are monogamous, some are more open, expanding to include affection or sexual activity with others. At the same time, there are thousands of single people who are still searching, waiting for that special someone to share their lives. Is there a particular approach to pursuing relationships we should be focusing on?"

The answer is plain. First of all, there are many different ways of relating, and simply being single doesn't imply dissatisfaction. We're not about to give a stamp of approval for any particular kind of lifestyle. There are all kinds of associations that serve people's unique needs. We've known people in stable relationships that include nonmonogamous behavior; threesomes; stable partnerships where one or the other may travel and indulge in anonymous sex; and unattached people who are looking for a partner and who devote a lot of time and energy to what might look like promiscuity.

Friendship First Is the Key

For those of you who have had one bad experience after another, it's time to concentrate on friendship first, sex later. Friendship delivers what sex promises, but fails to provide. It does appear that a lot of promiscuity among both gays and straights alike is related to a fear of intimacy.

There are all kinds of ways of associating or not associating that work for people at various stages of human development, but we can say unequivocally that no relationship works when friendship is missing. While this statement may seem rather unyielding, this reality has been proven time and again. The ideal match, of course, would be for you to fall in love with a true friend who also has the chemistry to light your fire, but *friendship* is the key ingredient, not love, not chemistry, because it's only a few lucky rascals who accidentally stumble into a combination of friendship and chemistry. The rest of us have to do some work to get there. So let's take a look at what it takes to nurture a friendship. That's the key. Knowing how to generate a friendship will give people the tools they need to form an enduring relationship with whatever chemical match they happen to pair up with.

Love the Person

There was an excellent and moving HBO television movie, written and directed by Jane Anderson and starring two Oscar-nominated actors, Jessica Lange and Tom Wilkinson. The show was called *Normal* and told of a married couple who "go through impossible circumstances and come out the other end." In it, Rob, a man who had been married for more than twenty years, confesses to Irma, his wife, that he never really felt whole. "I'm a man in a woman's body," he tearfully explains. "I'm the wrong gender. I'm really a woman."

At first she is horrified and throws him out of the house. Her minister and friends comfort her and urge her to get a divorce. Their son is understandably upset, although Rob and Irma's pre-teen daughter thinks "it's cool." Little by little, however, Irma begins to realize that she misses her husband's friendship. She tells her minister, "He's my heart." She begins to support Rob as he makes the gender transformation into Ruth. Irma understands that she had fallen in love with the person, not his sexuality. Far-fetched, you may think, but the underlying message is clear. True friendship is what's important in life.

Look at the friends you know. What do you see? There is definitely something about shared experiences. Friends enjoy doing things together. Beyond that, there's also a sense of adventure in spending time together. Friendship means treating each other with respect, relating to each other as equals, sharing important values and ideals. Friends are also individuals, people with individual identities. In a genuine friendship, two remain two. They certainly can and do have common passions and interests, but they also have their own lives, unique and separate preferences and talents.

Share the Virtues of Friendship

Author Ken Gross says: "True friends are bound together by altruism, kindness, and uncluttered generosity." Honesty and trust are also critical. Can you imagine a friendship in which people routinely deceive each other? It just wouldn't work. And don't forget a sense of humor. One of the most important ingredients is humor, not giddy silliness or practical jokes, but rather a kind of lightness, an ease in being with each other. "That is the best," said Gloria Vanderbilt, "to laugh because you both think the same things are funny." So many potential conflicts are easily diffused with a little humor. A little humor can lighten a situation and help another to realize it's time to also "lighten up."

No One Is Perfect

Finally, as author and gay activist Brian McNaught writes: "What we all probably know in our hearts but fail to acknowledge, is that there is no 'perfect person' awaiting our arrival and that no orgasm has much significance outside of a relationship. Each person is flawed in some way, but has the potential to be a wonderful friend and lover. Each sexual experience outside of a relationship is like a whiff of poppers or a toke of grass. They frequently provide momentary pleasure, but they are only a distraction from the real need to love and be loved."

Conclusion

"If I'm not for myself, who will be for me?
If I'm only for myself, what am I?
If not now, when?"

—The great Jewish sage, Hillel

THROUGHOUT THIS BOOK, we've tried to help guide you in your search for friendship, companionship, and love. But we have no magical formula. Don't get discouraged if you haven't, as yet, found someone special in your life. There are thousands of others just like you, also searching through the maze of time commitments, fears, self-doubts, and old tapes from well-meaning family and friends. Even if you run into a few dead ends and stumble at times, we believe you'll find companionship and love as you successfully find your way out of the labyrinth.

Keep in mind that you should . . .

- Always focus on friendship first, for that must be the foundation of any relationship.
- Be willing to try new adventures, take classes, and meet new people.
- Select activities that you enjoy because if you're happy with what you're doing, you'll reflect that attitude to the people you meet.

- Remember that you're never too old to enjoy physical contact, be it sexual or just cuddling.
- Be honest in your relationships because lies will come back to haunt you.
- Balance time for yourself with the time you spend with another.
- Move slowly if you're thinking of living with another person.
- Keep your sense of humor, for laughter cures a lot of ills.
- Accept faults in your friends because no one, including you, is perfect.
- Listen to your instincts and avoid dangerous situations.
- Remember your past, but don't dwell on it.
- Take your time because there's no deadline for love.

Good luck. May you find many friends and a special one as well.

> "There is something alarming about love, but friendship is forever our guardian angel."
>
> —Owen Dodson, poet

Suggested Reading

You'll find many nonfiction books that you may find helpful to read. Some of them are listed below:

The American Druggist's Complete Family Guide to Prescriptions, Pills, and Drugs. New York: Hearst Books, 1995.

Benson, Herbert, M.D. *The Break-Out Principle.* New York: Scribner, 2003.

Benson, Herbert, M.D. *The Relaxation Response.* New York: Quill, 2001.

Blank, Joani, Ed. *Still Doing It: Women and Men Over 60 Write about Their Sexuality.* San Francisco: Down There Press, 2000.

Boder, Michael S. *The Art of Living Single.* New York: Avon; Reprint edition, 1990.

Brooks, Gary R. and Glenn E. Good, Eds. *The New Handbook of Psychotherapy and Counseling with Men.* San Francisco, Calif.: Jossey-Bass, 2001.

Buber, Martin. *The Way of Man.* Secaucus, N.J.: Citadel Press, 1966.

Bullough, Vera L. and Bonnie Bullough. *Human Sexuality.* New York: Garland Pub., 1994.

Butler, Robert N. and Myra I. Lewis. *The New Love and Sex After 60.* New York: Ballantine Books, 2002.

Carter, Steven, and Julia Sokol. *Men Like Women Who Like Themselves.* New York: Delacorte Press, 1996.

Cassell, Carol. *Straight from the Heart.* New York: Simon & Schuster, 1987.

Colton, Helen. *The Gift of Touch.* New York: Seaview/Putnam, 1983.

Cousins, Norman. *Anatomy of an Illness.* Boston: G. K. Hall, 1980.

Cowens, Deborah. *A Gift for Healing.* New York: Crown Trade Paperbacks, 1996.

The Dalai Lama and Howard C Cutler. *The Art of Happiness.* New York: Riverhead Books, 1998.

DeAngelis, Barbara. *Are You the One for Me?* New York: Dell Publishing, 1992.

Dodson, Betty. *Liberating Masturbation.* New York, Dodson, 1976.

Doress-Worters, Paula Brown and Diana Laskin Siegal. *Ourselves Growing Older.* New York: Simon & Schuster, 1994.

Ellis, Albert, and Ted Crawford. *Making Intimate Connections.* Atascadero, Calif.: Impact Publishers, 2000.

Epstein, Mark. *Thoughts Without a Thinker.* New York, Oh.: MJF Books, 2003.

Frankl, Viktor E. *Man's Search for Meaning.* Boston: Beacon Press, 2000.

Friedan, Betty. *The Feminine Mystique.* Updated edition. New York: Norton, 2001.

Friedan, Betty. *The Fountain of Age.* New York: Simon & Schuster, 1993.

Fromm, Erich. *The Art of Loving.* New York: Continuum, 2000.

Galician, Mary-Lou. *Sex, Love, and Romance in the Mass Media.* Mahwah, N.J.: Lawrence Erlbaum Associates, 2004.

Galician, Mary-Lou. *Dr. Galician's Prescriptions for Getting Real about Romance: How Mass Media Myths about Love Can Hurt You.* Mahwah, N.J.: Lawrence Erlbaum Associates, 2004.

Glass, Shirley. *Not Just Friends: Protect Your Relationship from Infidelity and Heal the Trauma of Betrayal.* New York: Free Press, 2003.

Goldman, Daniel. *Destructive Emotions.* New York: Bantam Books, 2003.

Gordon, Sol. *How Can You Tell If You're Really in Love?* Avon, Mass.: Adams Media, 2001.

Gordon, Sol. *Why Love Is Not Enough.* Avon, Mass.: Adams Media, 1988.

Grimbol, William R., and Jeffrey Astrachan. *Life's Big Questions.* Indianapolis, In.: Alpha Books, 2002.

Harrison, Barbara. *50+ and Looking for Love Online.* Freedom, Calif.: The Crossing Press. 2000.

The Johns Hopkins Medical Guide to Health After 50. Simeon Margolis, ed. New York: Rebus, 2002.

Kennedy, Randall. *Interracial Intimacies.* New York: Pantheon, 2003.

Klein, Marty. *Beyond Orgasm—Dare to Be Honest about the Sex You Really Want.* Berkeley, Calif.: Celestial Arts, 2002.

Kushner, Harold. *Living a Life That Matters*. New York: A. A. Knopf, 2001.

Love, Pat. *The Truth about Love*. New York: Simon & Schuster, 2001.

Manheim, Camryn. *Wake Up, I'm Fat*. New York: Broadway Books, 1999.

Maslow, A. H. *Motivation and Personality*. New York: Harper and Row, 1987.

McCarthy, Barry and Emily. *Rekindling Desire: A Step-by-Step Program to Help Low-Sex and No-Sex Marriages*. New York: Brunner-Routledge, 2003.

O'Hanlon, Bill, and Pat Hudson. *Love Is a Verb*. New York: W.W. Norton, 1995.

O'Neil, Nena and George. *Open Marriage*. New York: M. Evans, 1972.

Peale, Norman Vincent. *The Power of Positive Thinking*. New York: Fireside/Simon & Schuster, 2003.

Peale, Norman Vincent. *You Can If You Think You Can*. Pawling, N.Y.: Foundation for Christian Living, 1984.

Peck, M. Scott. *The Road Less Traveled*. Kansas City, Mo.: Andrews McMeel Publishing, 2001.

Perry, Susan K. *Loving in Flow*. Naperville, Ill.: Sourcebooks Casablanca, 2003.

Prather, Hugh. *Notes to Myself*. New York: Bantam Books, 1990.

Real, Terrance. *How Can I Get Through to You?* New York: Scribner, 2002.

Real, Terrance. *I Don't Want to Talk about It*. New York: Fireside, 1998.

Reichman, Judith. *I'm Too Young to Get Old*. New York: Times Books, 1996.

Rosenberg, Helena Hacker. *How to Get Married After 35*. New York: HarperCollinsPublishers, 1998.

Schnarch, David. *Passionate Marriage*. New York: Henry Holt, 1998.

Shimberg, Elaine Fantle. *Blending Families*. New York: Berkley Books, 1999.

Solot, Dorian, and Marshall Miller. *Unmarried to Each Other*. New York: Marlowe: distributed by Publishers Group West, 2002.

Suib Cohen, Sherry. *The Magic of Touch*. New York: Harper & Row, 1987.

Tessina, Tina. *The Unofficial Guide to Dating Again.* New York: John Wiley & Sons, 1999.

Viorst, Judith. *Grown Up Marriage.* New York: Free Press, 2003.

Viorst, Judith. *Necessary Losses.* New York: Simon & Schuster, 1986.

Weiner-Davis, Michele. *The Sex-Starved Marriage.* New York: Simon & Schuster, 2003.

Welles, Paddy S. *To Stand in Love.* Alliance House, 2000.

These are novels that deal with the purpose of life:

Hesse, Hermann. *Siddhartha.* Boston: Shambhala, 2002.

Kosinski, Jerzy. *The Painted Bird.* New Brunswick, N.J.: Transaction Publishers, 2000.

Kundera, Milan. *The Book of Laughter and Forgetting.* New York: HarperPerennial, 1996.

Matthiessen, Peter. *The Snow Leopard.* New York: Penguin Books, 1996.

Walker, Alice. *The Color Purple.* Orlando, Fla.: Harcourt, 2003.

We also recommend novels by Tim O'Brian, Russell Banks, E. L. Doctorow, Kurt Vonnegut, Sholem Asch, Albert Camus, Franz Kafka, Erica Yong, Herbert Melville, Anne Tyler, Cynthia Ozick, John Steinbeck, James Baldwin, Thomas Mann, Saul Bellow, Virginia Woolf, Isaac Bashevis Singer, Ernest Hemmingway, and Eli Wiesel. Which others would *you* suggest?

Try rereading old favorites—novels by Tolstoy, Dostoevsky, Proust, Brontë, Hugo, Joyce, Wharton, Cather, Dickens, and, of course, William Shakespeare. Also there are plays by Beckett, Chekhov, Ibsen, and Wilde, and poetry by Dickinson. You may have studied these in school years ago, but you're bound to get more out of them today.

Russell Baker's autobiography, *Growing Up* (Thorndike, Me.: Thorndike Press, 1982), is inspirational as is Tom Brokaw's *Long Way from Home* (New York: Random House, 2002) and Eudora Welty's *One Writer's Beginnings* (New York: Warner Books, 1991).

If you're not into reading or it's difficult to read for any length of time, consider audiotapes.

Index